# WORD FOR WINDOWS 6 FOR DUMMIES™

## *Quick Reference*

## by George T. Lynch

**IDG BOOKS**

IDG Books Worldwide, Inc.
An International Data Group Company

San Mateo, California ♦ Indianapolis, Indiana ♦ Boston, Massachusetts

# Word For Windows 6 For Dummies Quick Reference

Published by
**IDG Books Worldwide, Inc.**
An International Data Group Company
155 Bovet Road, Suite 310
San Mateo, CA 94402

Library of Congress Catalog Card No.: 93-81198

ISBN: 1-56884-095-0

Printed in the United States of America

10 9 8 7 6 5 4 3 2 1

Distributed in the United States by IDG Books Worldwide, Inc.

Distributed in Canada by Macmillan of Canada, a Division of Canada Publishing Corporation; by Computer and Technical Books in Miami, Florida, for South America and the Caribbean; by Longman Singapore in Singapore, Malaysia, Thailand, and Korea; by Toppan Co. Ltd. in Japan; by Asia Computerworld in Hong Kong; by Woodslane Pty. Ltd. in Australia and New Zealand; and by Transword Publishers Ltd. in the U.K. and Europe.

For information on where to purchase IDG Books outside the U.S., contact Christina Turner at 415-312-0633.

For information on translations, contact Marc Jeffrey Mikulich, Foreign Rights Manager, at IDG Books Worldwide; FAX NUMBER 415-358-1260.

For sales inquiries and special prices for bulk quantities, write to the address above or call IDG Books Worldwide at 415-312-0650.

# Acknowledgments

As much as I would like to believe that I wrote this book, it is really the result of a team of people who supported, prodded, urged, and otherwise helped me in so many ways. I would be an ingrate not to try to mention as many of them as possible. I have to start with my wife, Maureen, who bore with me and, as always, lent moral and other support during this project. Major thanks also to my friend and colleague, Don Gosselin, who willingly gave of his extensive knowledge and offered many invaluable suggestions. I must also thank Belinda Rubino and Pam Holland for their patience and good humor. Others who contributed in one form or another include Michael Dagley, Steve Ryan, Pico Nazzaro, Juancho Ciocon and Mark Read, all of First Boston's fine technical support team. (I also want to thank other members of First Boston's support team, but they are too numerous to mention by name here.) Other names I'd like to mention include Billy Jira, Raymond Tracey, Joe Ganatello, Tom Monteforte, and Mike Lynch, my brother. I don't want to forget Harlan Lax for his advice on this and other books. And I have been remiss in the past for not acknowledging Brian Livingston, who was instrumental in helping me begin to write.

I also want to thank David Solomon and Janna Custer for the opportunity to do this book. I will also always remember Diane Steele, my editor, for her gentle and not-so-gentle prodding. Thanks to Sara Black and John Kaufeld for the copy and technical editing of the book. Thanks also to Mary Bednarek for her encouragement. And I'd like to give a special mention to all the other fine folk at IDG (Leigh Davis and Megg Bonnar especially).

## Credits

**Publisher**
David Solomon

**Managing Editor**
Mary Bednarek

**Acquisitions Editor**
Janna Custer

**Production Director**
Beth Jenkins

**Senior Editors**
Tracy L. Barr
Sandy Blackthorn
Diane Graves Steele

**Production Coordinator**
Cindy L. Phipps

**Acquisitions Assistant**
Megg Bonar

**Editorial Assistant**
Darlene Cunningham

**Editor**
Sara Black

**Technical Reviewer**
John Kaufeld

**Production Staff**
Tony Augsburger
Valery Bourke
Mary Breidenbach
Chris Collins
Sherry Gomoll
Drew Moore
Kathie Schnorr
Gina Scott

**Proofreader**
Sandy Grieshop

# Say What You Think!

Listen up, all you readers of IDG's international bestsellers: the one — the only — absolutely world famous *...For Dummies* books! It's time for you to take advantage of a new, direct pipeline to the authors and editors of IDG Books Worldwide. In between putting the finishing touches on the next round of *...For Dummies* books, the authors and editors of IDG Books Worldwide like to sit around and mull over what their readers have to say. And we know that you readers always say what you think. So here's your chance. We'd really like your input for future printings and editions of this book — and ideas for future *...For Dummies* titles as well. Tell us what you liked (and didn't like) about this book. How about the chapters you found most useful — or most funny? And since we know you're not a bit shy, what about the chapters you think can be improved? Just to show you how much we appreciate your input, we'll add you to our Dummies Database/Fan Club and keep you up to date on the latest *...For Dummies* books, news, cartoons, calendars, and more! Please send your name, address, and phone number, as well as your comments, questions, and suggestions, to our very own *...For Dummies* coordinator at the following address:

**...For Dummies Coordinator**
IDG Books Worldwide
3250 North Post Road, Suite 140
Indianapolis, IN 46226

(Yes, Virginia, there really is a *...For Dummies* coordinator. We are not making this up.)

Please mention the name of this book in your comments.

Thanks for your input!

# *About IDG Books Worldwide*

Welcome to the world of IDG Books Worldwide.

IDG Books Worldwide, Inc., is a division of International Data Group, the world's largest publisher of computer-related information and the leading global provider of information services on information technology. IDG publishes over 194 computer publications in 62 countries. Forty million people read one or more IDG publications each month.

If you use personal computers, IDG Books is committed to publishing quality books that meet your needs. We rely on our extensive network of publications, including such leading periodicals as *Macworld, InfoWorld, PC World, Publish, Computerworld, Network World,* and *SunWorld,* to help us make informed and timely decisions in creating useful computer books that meet your needs.

Every IDG book strives to bring extra value and skill-building instruction to the reader. Our books are written by experts, with the backing of IDG periodicals, and with careful thought devoted to issues such as audience, interior design, use of icons, and illustrations. Our editorial staff is a careful mix of high-tech journalists and experienced book people. Our close contact with the makers of computer products helps ensure accuracy and thorough coverage. Our heavy use of personal computers at every step in production means we can deliver books in the most timely manner.

We are delivering books of high quality at competitive prices on topics customers want. At IDG, we believe in quality, and we have been delivering quality for over 25 years. You'll find no better book on a subject than an IDG book.

John Kilcullen
President and C.E.O.
IDG Books Worldwide, Inc.

IDG Books Worldwide, Inc. is a division of International Data Group. The officers are Patrick J. McGovern, Founder and Board Chairman; Walter Boyd, President. International Data Group's publications include: **ARGENTINA's** Computerworld Argentina, InfoWorld Argentina; **ASIA's** Computerworld Hong Kong, PC World Hong Kong, Computerworld Southeast Asia, PC World Singapore, Computerworld Malaysia, PC World Malaysia; **AUSTRALIA's** Computerworld Australia, Australian PC World, Australian Macworld, Network World, Reseller, IDG Sources; **AUSTRIA's** Computerwelt Oesterreich, PC Test; **BRAZIL's** Computerworld, Mundo IBM, Mundo Unix, PC World, Publish; **BULGARIA's** Computerworld Bulgaria, Ediworld, PC & Mac World Bulgaria; **CANADA's** Direct Access, Graduate Computerworld, InfoCanada, Network World Canada; **CHILE's** Computerworld, Informatica; **COLOMBIA's** Computerworld Colombia; **CZECH REPUBLIC's** Computerworld, Elektronika, PC World; **DENMARK's** CAD/CAM WORLD, Communications World, Computerworld Danmark, LOTUS World, Macintosh Produktkatalog, Macworld Danmark, PC World Danmark, PC World Produktguide, Windows World; **EQUADOR's** PC World; **EGYPT's** Computerworld (CW) Middle East, PC World Middle East; **FINLAND's** MikroPC, Tietoviikko, Tietoverkko; **FRANCE's** Distributique, GOLDEN MAC, InfoPC, Languages & Systems, Le Guide du Monde Informatique, Le Monde Informatique, Telecoms & Reseaux; **GERMANY's** Computerwoche, Computerwoche Focus, Computerwoche Extra, Computerwoche Karriere, Information Management, Macwelt, Netzwelt, PC Welt, PC Woche, Publish, Unit; **HUNGARY's** Alaplap, Computerworld SZT, PC World, ; **INDIA's** Computers & Communications; **ISRAEL's** Computerworld Israel, PC World Israel; **ITALY's** Computerworld Italia, Lotus Magazine, Macworld Italia, Networking Italia, PC World Italia; **JAPAN's** Computerworld Japan, Macworld Japan, SunWorld Japan, Windows World; **KENYA's** East African Computer News; **KOREA's** Computerworld Korea, Macworld Korea, PC World Korea; **MEXICO's** Compu Edicion, Compu Manufactura, Computacion/Punto de Venta, Computerworld Mexico, MacWorld, Mundo Unix, PC World, Windows; **THE NETHERLAND'S** Computer! Totaal, LAN Magazine, MacWorld; **NEW ZEALAND's** Computer Listings, Computerworld New Zealand, New Zealand PC World; **NIGERIA's** PC World Africa; **NORWAY's** Computerworld Norge, C/World, Lotusworld Norge, Macworld Norge, Networld, PC World Ekspress, PC World Norge, PC World's Product Guide, Publish World, Student Data, Unix World, Windowsworld, IDG Direct Response; **PANAMA's** PC World; **PERU's** Computerworld Peru, PC World; **PEOPLES REPUBLIC OF CHINA's** China Computerworld, PC World China, Electronics International, China Network World; **IDG HIGH TECH BEIJING's** New Product World; **IDG SHENZHEN's** Computer News Digest; **PHILLIPPINES'** Computerworld, PC World; **POLAND's** Computerworld Poland, PC World/ Komputer; **PORTUGAL's** Cerebro/PC World, Correio Informatico/Computerworld, MacIn; **ROMANIA's** PC World; **RUSSIA's** Computerworld-Moscow, Mir-PC, Sety; **SLOVENIA's** Monitor Magazine; **SOUTH AFRICA's** Computing S.A.; **SPAIN's** Amiga World, Computerworld Espana, Communicaciones World, Macworld Espana, NeXTWORLD, PC World Espana, Publish, Sunworld; **SWEDEN's** Attack, ComputerSweden, Corporate Computing, Lokala Natverk/LAN, Lotus World, MAC&PC, Macworld, Mikrodatorn, PC World, Publishing & Design (CAP), Datalngenjoren, Maxi Data, Windows World; **SWITZERLAND's** Computerworld Schweiz, Macworld Schweiz, PC & Workstation; **TAIWAN's** Computerworld Taiwan, Global Computer Express, PC World Taiwan; **THAILAND's** Thai Computerworld; **TURKEY's** Computerworld Monitor, Macworld Turkiye, PC World Turkiye; **UNITED KINGDOM's** Lotus Magazine, Macworld; **UNITED STATES'** AmigaWorld, Cable in the Classroom, CD Review, CIO, Computerworld, Desktop Video World, DOS Resource Guide, Electronic News, Federal Computer Week, Federal Integrator, GamePro, IDG Books, InfoWorld, InfoWorld Direct, Laser Event, Macworld, Multimedia World, Network World, NeXTWORLD, PC Games, PC Letter, PC World Publish, Sumeria, SunWorld, SWATPro, Video Event; **VENEZUELA's** Computerworld Venezuela, MicroComputerworld Venezuela; **VIETNAM's** PC World Vietnam

# About the Author

George Lynch, the author of several computer books, has been a computer training and development consultant in the New York City area for the past several years. His clients have included major investment and commercial banks, law firms, real estate companies, smaller businesses, and individuals. He is a certified professional in Windows, Word for Windows, and Excel. He has written numerous training manuals, articles, and user guides for clients. He is co-president of the New Yord Word for Windows Business Users Group and is on the board of directors of the New York Amateur Computer Club.

## Contents at a Glance

## Word For Windows 6, a word processing system that combines ease of use with power

Welcome to the Word For Windows 6 For Dummies Quick Reference, a guide that takes you through the most commonly used features of Word for Windows 6.

When you get to know this version of Word for Windows you will surely agree that it was designed with convenience and ease of use in mind. From the rich quality-of-life features (like AutoCorrect and the automatic description of buttons on the toolbar) to the most powerful features (like styles, tables and macros), Word For Windows is a pleasure to use.

The best way to learn Word for Windows is to experiment. You can learn a lot more about a feature by trying it and making mistakes than by reading about it. And, because Word For Windows has a multiple Undo feature, you can't really hurt yourself much. Just keep clicking that Undo button until you've finally undone that nasty thing that caused you so much grief.

Each topic in this book is handled in a similar fashion. There is a one or two line description of what the feature does, followed by a more detailed explanation of the feature. Then there are step-by-step instructions on using that feature. Some topics include shortcut keystrokes (For Keyboard Kutups) and shortcut mouse actions (For Mouse Maniacs). This is followed in most cases by a "More Stuff" section where you'll find tips, warnings and reminders about that feature.

## How Do I Use This Book?

Because this book is an alphabetical reference, you can easily find the feature or task you are seeking — just use it like a dictionary and look up the first letter! The running heads will help point you to the location of the primary entries, too.

Each feature and function is presented with a suitability and safety icon to let you know how regularly you are likely to use it and how safe your data is likely to be when you use it. The book uses a variety of other icons too (see "The Cast of Icons") so that you can see at a glance what to avoid and what might be safe and helpful. If you are like most users of word processing systems, your approach is to try something and if it doesn't work, panic. Let me suggest that you first consult this Quick Reference. You'll find that you can reduce the frequency of errors *and* reduce the amount and intensity of your panic.

## The Cast Of Icons

The following icons appear throughout this book to help point out important information. They instantly tell you a few key things about each feature.

 Probably worth your while to learn about this one.

 Normally used only by advanced Word for Windows 6 users or for special purposes; can be useful at times.

 Generally not used by beginners, but you may have to do this anyway.

 Indicates that this operation is safe for your data (worst case is another error message).

 Generally safe in most circumstances, unless you don't follow instructions (then look out!).

 Potentially dangerous to data but necessary in the scheme of things; *be careful* with this one.

 A problem area that can mess up your work if you don't stay on your toes; something in this one can get you in trouble.

 Alerts you to a way of using a command that may not be immediately obvious to average users.

 A little information that can be stored away deep inside your brain.

 Look out! Even if this one says *Safe* or *Generally Safe*, there's a little something here that can cause you trouble.

 Flags cross references to other areas of this book that might be of interest to you.

 Tells you to look in *Word For Windows 6 For Dummies* for more information.

# The Word For Windows 6 Quick Reference

## Abbreviations

You can use Abbreviations for standard (boilerplate) text and graphics that you use frequently in your documents.

To insert text in place of your abbreviations automatically as you type, see **AutoCorrect.** To type a code in order to retrieve large amounts of text and graphics, see **AutoText** (formerly Glossaries).

## Alignment

Aligns paragraphs as you specify: left, right, center, or justified. To use this command, you must be sure that the insertion point is in the paragraph. If you want to align more than one consecutive paragraph, select them first.

### Applying Alignment to selected paragraphs

1. Choose Format⇨Paragraph to open the Paragraph dialog box.
2. Click the Indents and Spacing tab.
3. Click in the list box under Alignment (lower right of window) to see all the choices.
4. Make your choice and click OK.

### For keyboard kut-ups

To left align a paragraph, press

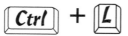

To right align a paragraph, press

**Ctrl** + **R**

To center a paragraph between the margins, press

**Ctrl** + **E**

To fully justify a paragraph, press

**Ctrl** + **J**

## For mouse maniacs

Click one of the alignment buttons on the Formatting toolbar. From left to right, they represent left, center, right, and justified.

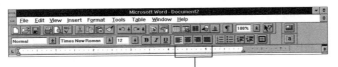

Paragraph alignment buttons

## More stuff

Don't be confused by the fact that Microsoft uses Ctrl+E to center a paragraph. They actually had a pretty good reason for this choice: They used Ctrl+C as the keyboard shortcut for the **Copy** command instead. The choice seems reasonable to me.

Alignment is based on the margins, not on the page size. So if you try to center something and it doesn't appear centered when you print, check your margins — they probably aren't equal.

## All Caps

Converts text to all caps. You can apply this command again to the same text to convert it to its original upper- and lowercase formatting. Although you can use the Font dialog box to get the same results, using the keystroke combination is far easier.

## Applying All Caps

1. Choose Format➪Font to open the Font dialog box.

2. Click the Font tab.

3. Under Effects, enable <u>A</u>ll Caps and click OK.

## *For keyboard kut-ups*

Select the text and press

## *More stuff*

You can use this command to apply and remove All Caps formatting. It has no effect, however, on text you type using the Shift key or with Caps Lock on.

---

## Anchoring Objects to Paragraphs

Anchors a framed object to a specific paragraph. When you frame an object, you can move it to any position on the page. Word anchors the framed object to the closest paragraph. However, you can anchor and lock the framed object to any paragraph on the page so that the object stays with that paragraph, even if the paragraph moves to another page. You can see the anchor when you are in Page Layout view, the Showall button on the Standard toolbar is enabled, and the framed object is selected.

## *Framed object anchored to closest paragraph*

## *Seeing the anchor*

Remember that you must start with a framed object. If you don't have a framed object, this command won't work.

1. Choose <u>V</u>iew⇨<u>P</u>age Layout to switch to Page Layout view.

2. Select the framed object.

3. Enable the Showall button on the Standard toolbar. The anchor appears to the left of the paragraph that is closest to the object.

Show all button

## *Lifting anchor*

To move the anchor to a different paragraph, follow the steps to make the anchor appear. Then drag the anchor to the paragraph to which you want to anchor the framed object. That's all there is to it.

## *Locking the anchor*

Locking an anchor means that the anchor stays attached to a specific paragraph even if you move the framed object. (Remember that Word normally anchors a framed object to the closest paragraph. If you move either the object or the paragraph, the anchor moves to the next closest paragraph.) You should lock the anchor to a specific paragraph when you want the framed object to appear on the same page as that paragraph.

When you lock the anchor, you can drag the object anywhere on the page and have no effect on the anchor or the paragraph. However, if the anchored paragraph moves to another page because of editing, the object moves with it. The object appears in the same spot on the new page as it did on the old page, but it is still anchored to the same paragraph (regardless of where the paragraph itself sits on the page).

1. Follow the steps to see the anchor.

2. Double-click the anchor to open the Frame dialog box or choose Format⇨Frame from the menu.

3. Click the Lock Anchor option in the Vertical section. When an X appears in the box, the anchor is locked and a small lock appears next to the anchor when it is visible.

## *More stuff*

Anchoring is a part of framing, which is how you position objects on the page. For more on this topic, see **Framing.**

For more information on anchoring and framing, see **Framing** in *Word For Windows 6 For Dummies.*

## Annotations

Lets reviewers make electronic comments on a document. Have you ever circulated a draft of a large document so that everyone in the company could comment on it and mark it up? Then, when everyone had seen it, you tried your best to make sense of all those scribbles and notes. Now you can use Word's Annotations feature instead of the old draft copy. Annotations consist of the annotation reference mark that you put in your text (like a footnote except the annotation reference mark isn't always visible) and the annotation itself. When you create or view an annotation, the Annotation pane opens for you to work in.

## Inserting an annotation

1. Position the insertion point where you want the annotation reference mark to appear.

2. Choose Insert⇨Annotation to insert the reference mark in the text and open the Annotation pane (see the following annotation example).

3. Type the annotation comments.

4. Click the Close button to close the Annotation pane.

Word automatically numbers annotations as you insert them. If you insert a new annotation before an existing one in a document, Word automatically renumbers them all correctly.

## For keyboard kut-ups

To open the Annotation pane, position the insertion point and press

Then, type the annotation and click the Close button.

## Annotation example

## *Viewing an annotation*

Remember that viewing an annotation is different from viewing an annotation reference mark. The annotation is the comment about the document. The annotation reference mark indicates where in the document the annotation is placed.

Annotation reference marks are formatted as hidden text and thus are not generally visible. You can view your annotation reference marks in several ways. For example, you can click the Showall button on the Standard toolbar to show all nonprinting characters or choose Tools⇨Options, click the View tab to open the View Options dialog box, and choose Hidden Text under Nonprinting Characters.

Annotation reference marks also become visible when you view the annotations in the document. Choose View⇨Annotation to open the Annotation pane.

## *Deleting an annotation*

As with footnotes, you cannot delete an annotation itself. Instead, you must delete the annotation reference mark in the text. You may be happy to know that Word automatically renumbers all the remaining annotations automatically.

1. Choose View⇨Annotation to open the Annotation pane and make the annotation reference marks visible.

2. In the Annotation pane, click the annotation you want to delete. When you select a specific annotation, Word shades the annotation reference mark in the text and makes it visible on the screen. (Word shades the reference mark to make it easy for you to see. This does not mean that Word selected the reference mark; you must select the mark separately.)

3. Click the document portion of the screen above the Annotation pane to make the document active.

4. Select the annotation reference mark and press Delete. Either click and drag with the mouse or use Shift and an arrow key to highlight the code. Don't double-click it — that takes you back to the annotation window. The annotation reference mark and the annotation disappear. Word renumbers the remaining annotations automatically.

5. Click back in the Annotation pane and follow steps 1 through 4 to delete additional annotations.

## *Changing the annotator's initials*

Word takes the annotator's initials from User Info.

1. Choose Tools⇨Options to open the Options dialog box.

2. Click the User Info tab.

3. In the Initials section, type the initials you want to use for annotations and click OK.

## Printing annotations

For more on printing options, see **Printing.**

You can print your annotations, with or without your document.

1. Choose File⇨Print to open the Print dialog box.

2. Click the Print What box to see more options. Choose Annotations to print the annotations instead of the document.

3. To print both the document and the annotations, leave Document selected in the Print What box and click the Options button to open the Print Options dialog box. Under Include With Document, click Annotations and then click OK to return to the Print dialog box.

4. Click OK to print whatever you selected.

## More stuff

You can also go to a specific annotation by pressing F5 to open the GoTo dialog box. (For more on moving around your document, see **GoTo.**) Choose Annotation in the Go To What box, and you can choose a specific reviewer or any reviewer. Even if the Showall button is not enabled, Word takes you to the reference mark although it is not visible, but you still need to enable the Showall button to see the reference mark.

When nonprinting characters are visible, you can see the annotation reference marks in your document. You can quickly open the Annotation pane by double-clicking any annotation reference mark. When the pane opens, the insertion point appears in front of the annotation that corresponds to the annotation reference mark on which you double-clicked.

For more on this topic, see the chapter on Annotations in *Word For Windows 6 For Dummies.*

## AutoCorrect

Corrects listed spelling errors automatically as you type. According to many users, AutoCorrect is one of the nicest features in Word. It is nothing more than a table where you list your most common spelling errors and their correct spelling. When the AutoCorrect table is enabled, Word automatically corrects any spelling errors listed in the table. No intervention from the user is necessary. How about that?

Naturally, you might want to expand on this wonderful feature. So, instead of listing just spelling errors, you can also abbreviate phrases you don't like typing, like complicated medical and legal phrases, foreign phrases, and corporate names. For example, if you tell Word that when you type **MJF** you want it to enter the law firm name of **McGillicuddy, Jacobsen, FitzOwens, Smythe, and McWilliams.** Then, every time you type **MJF**, Word inserts the full name of the law firm.

## Using AutoCorrect

1. Choose <u>T</u>ools⇨AutoCorrect to open  AutoCorrect dialog box.

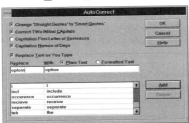

2. Choose the options and enter any new AutoCorrect items you want.

3. After you make your choices, click OK.

4. To use AutoCorrect, just type and make an error that is listed in the AutoCorrect dialog box. The error is corrected automatically.

## More stuff

If you open the AutoCorrect dialog box and enter text directly in the <u>R</u>eplace and <u>W</u>ith boxes, the <u>P</u>lain Text and <u>F</u>ormatted Text options aren't available. You can make them available by typing the correct word in your document, selecting it, and then opening the AutoCorrect dialog box. Word automatically inserts the word you select in the <u>W</u>ith box and enables the text options. The insertion point flashes in the <u>R</u>eplace box so that you can type the incorrect entry.

## AutoFormat

Automatically formats an entire document using styles from the attached template. You later have the opportunity to review and accept or reject each formatting change. You can also set specific options before using AutoFormat to limit the formatting performed by Word.

This feature is a quick and powerful method of applying styles and formatting your documents, but you need to watch out for some traps.

## Using AutoFormat

You can use AutoFormat in a number of different ways, including a couple of methods that don't give you the option of reviewing the changes. Until you become very familiar with templates, styles, and the AutoFormat feature, you should stay with the methods that allow you to review formatting changes (and thereby reject any unwanted changes). The following steps allow you to review any changes made by the AutoFormat feature.

1. Format⇨AutoFormat to open the AutoFormat dialog box. (There are actually two AutoFormat dialog boxes — one that appears before the AutoFormat and one that appears after it's done.)

2. Click the Options button to open the Options dialog box. Make your choices here. (For an explanation of each option in this dialog box, click the Help button.) When you finish, click OK to return to the AutoFormat dialog box.

3. Click OK or press Enter to begin. When the AutoFormat is complete, the second AutoFormat dialog box appears. It contains choices relating to the formatting just completed.

4. Click the Accept or Reject All button to accept or reject all the changes.

5. To review the individual changes, click the Review Changes button. This command opens the Review AutoFormat Changes dialog box. (You can also click the Style Gallery button to view and copy styles from a different template.)

6. Click the Find button with the arrow that points to the right to begin reviewing the changes. Word finds the first change and awaits your decision.

7. To accept the change, click the Find button again to move to the next change. To reject the change, click the Reject button. To move to the next change automatically after rejecting the current change, enable the Find Next after Reject option.

8. If you find the revision marks that Word uses to indicate changes distracting, click the Hide Marks button to hide them.

9. When you have completed reviewing the changes, the Cancel button becomes the Close button. Click this button to close the dialog box.

## Keyboard kut-ups

You can autoformat your document quickly by pressing

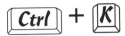

However, this method doesn't allow you to review your changes. If you don't like them, you must undo them by using the Undo command or modify the formatting paragraph by paragraph.

## For mouse maniacs

Click the AutoFormat button on the Standard toolbar to quickly autoformat your document. This method, like its keyboard shortcut cousin, does not permit you to review the changes Word makes to your document.

## More stuff

If you use the keyboard or mouse approach, you can always undo the changes by clicking the Undo button on the Standard toolbar. Another remedy is to close the document without saving the changes, but this may mean losing other changes as well.

Always save your document *before* doing this operation. Then if something goes horribly wrong, your document is still in good shape.

For more information on using styles with the AutoFormat feature in Word, see the chapter on Styles in *Word For Windows 6 For Dummies.*

## AutoText (formerly Glossary)

Allows you to store and use text and graphics as often as needed. This feature was known as the Glossary in previous versions of Word, and it still works essentially the same way: You select the text or graphics you want to store as an AutoText entry and then give the entry a code name. To retrieve the entry later, type the code name and press F3. There's nothing to it.

## Creating an AutoText entry

1. Select the text or graphic you want to add. The size of the entry is not limited; rather, it depends on your computer's configuration.

2. Choose Edit⇨AutoText to open the AutoText dialog box. Your selection (or a portion of it, depending on its size) shows in the Selection box at the bottom, and Word proposes a name in the Name box based on the selection.

3. Accept the proposed name or type another. Word allows up to 30 characters, including spaces and special characters, for AutoText names.

4. In the Make AutoText Entry Available To box, specify the template in which you want to store the AutoText entry. The default is All Documents, which makes the entry available to every document created in Word. If the current document is based on a custom template, you can choose that template instead.

5. Click the Add button to add the entry and close the dialog box.

## Keyboard kut-ups

To insert an AutoText entry in your document, type the AutoText entry code (name assigned to the AutoText entry) and press

## For mouse maniacs

To insert an AutoText entry in your document, type the AutoText entry code (the name assigned to the AutoText entry) and click the Insert AutoText button on the Standard toolbar.

## AutoText dialog box

The AutoText dialog box changes, depending on whether you choose something before you open it.

Selection

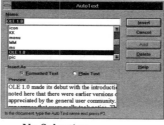
No Selection

## Inserting an AutoText entry

It is quicker and easier to use either the mouse or the keyboard method, but if you forget the AutoText code name for the entry you can use this method:

1. Position the insertion point where you want the entry to be inserted.

2. Choose Edit⇨AutoText to open the AutoText dialog box.

3. Scroll through the list of names in the Name box. When you select a name, the AutoText entry (or a portion of it) appears in the Preview box at the bottom of the dialog box.

4. Specify how you want the entry to be inserted, as plain or formatted text.

5. Click the Insert button to insert the entry and close the dialog box.

6. Click the Delete button to erase the selected entry from the AutoText list.

## More stuff

Word provides a related feature called the *Spike*. You can use the Spike to collect a number of entries at one time and then insert all the entries at once. See **Spike** for more on this topic.

You can use up to 30 characters to name an AutoText entry, including spaces. However, as a practical matter, you should keep the names as short as possible for those times when you type the name and press F3.

## *Block Protecting*

Prevents page breaks from occurring within a paragraph or between selected paragraphs. Strictly speaking, blocks and block commands aren't part of Word's lexicon, but they have become common terms in word processing. Word has two types of blocks: lines you want to keep together on a page and paragraphs you want to keep together on a page. Both are paragraph formatting commands.

For a description of the Paragraph dialog box, see **Paragraph Formatting.**

## Keeping lines and paragraphs together

Keeping lines together means preventing a page break from occurring within a paragraph. If a page break were to occur within the lines, Word would move the entire paragraph to the next page.

1. Select the paragraph that contains the lines you want to keep together.

2. Format⇨Paragraph to open the Paragraph dialog box.

3. Click the Text Flow tab.

4. To prevent a page break from occurring within a paragraph, enable the Keep Lines Together option under Pagination.

5. Click OK to close the dialog box.

Keeping paragraphs together prevents a page break from occurring between selected paragraphs. This option is commonly used to keep a text paragraph and its heading on the same page.

1. Click the first paragraph only.

2. Choose Format⇨Paragraph.

3. Click the Text Flow tab.

4. Enable the Keep With Next option.

5. Click OK to close the dialog box.

## More stuff

Blocking is generally safe, but you can easily forget that some paragraphs are blocked when you paginate your document. Also, it is possible to turn on these options as you type and forget to turn them off, causing strange pagination errors. If you are confronted with pagination problems that seem unusual (like a page break after every paragraph), select one or two paragraphs and look at the Keep options in the Paragraph dialog box. They probably are in effect for the entire document. To correct the problem, clear these options for the entire document. You can enter them again for the correct paragraphs after you correct the pagination problem.

## Bold

Bolds selected text. Bolding is a character attribute, which means that you must select the character before you can bold it (unlike paragraph attributes for which you need only be in the paragraph). To turn off bolding, repeat the keyboard or toolbar action you use to turn it on.

## For keyboard kut-ups

Select the text and press

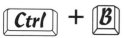

## *For mouse maniacs*

Select the text and click the Bold button on the Formatting toolbar.

See **Character Formatting** for more on this topic.

## *Bookmarks*

Mark text, graphics, or elements in your document. You can use bookmarks to jump to specific locations in a document (just like a real bookmark). You can also use bookmarks for cross-referencing within a document and for indicating a range of pages in an index. All in all, using bookmarks can be quite useful, especially in larger documents.

## *Creating a bookmark*

1. Select the text or item you want to define as a bookmark or just position the insertion point in your document to specify a place.

2. Choose Edit⇨Bookmark to open the Bookmark dialog box.

3. Type a name for the bookmark in the Bookmark Name box.

4. Click Add to add the bookmark and close the dialog box.

## *For keyboard kut-ups*

Press

$$\boxed{Ctrl} + \boxed{Shift} + \boxed{F5}$$

## *Jumping to a bookmark*

1. Press F5 to open the GoTo dialog box.

2. Under Go To What, choose Bookmark.

3. Click the down arrow to the right of the list box under <u>E</u>nter Bookmark Name to see all the bookmarks in the document.

4. Choose the bookmark you want to jump to and click Go<u>T</u>o.

5. Click Close to close the dialog box.

## Deleting a bookmark

1. Choose <u>E</u>dit⇨<u>B</u>ookmark to open the Bookmark dialog box.

2. Choose the bookmark you want to delete.

3. Click the <u>D</u>elete button. To delete another, choose it and click the <u>D</u>elete button again.

4. Click Close to close the dialog box.

## Seeing bookmarks

Bookmarks show up as large brackets surrounding whatever text or item you selected or as a single bracket if you didn't select anything before inserting the bookmark. If you insert a bookmark and you can't see the bracket(s) indicator, choose <u>T</u>ools⇨<u>O</u>ptions, click the View tab, and enable Boo<u>k</u>marks under Show.

## More stuff

Bookmark names must begin with a letter and can consist of no more than 40 characters. Word doesn't allow spaces in bookmark names, but you can use underscores for clarity. You can have up to 32,000 bookmarks in a Word 6 document (but why would you want to?).

If you copy all or part of a marked item to a different location in the same document, the bookmark stays with the original. Additionally, if you copy all or part of a marked item to a different document, the bookmark also appears in the other document.

Using bookmarks has no downside and several benefits. The major benefit is that you can jump instantly to a specific spot in your document regardless of what page it currently occupies.

## Borders and Shading

Adds borders and shading to selected text and tables. You cannot add shading to a graphic nor to a frame that contains a graphic, although you can add shading to a frame that contains text.

# Applying borders and shading

The easiest method for applying borders and shading is to use
the Borders toolbar.

However, if you want a shadowed box (the right and bottom
borders are thicker than the left and top borders) or if you want
to specify how far the border should be from the text, you must
use the Paragraph Borders and Shading dialog box.

1. Select the item you want to have a border. For example, if
   you want to add a border to a table, select the entire table.
   If you want to add a border to part of a table, select that
   part (row, column, cell, and so on).

2. Click the Borders button on the Formatting toolbar. The
   Borders toolbar opens.

3. Choose the line style for the border. The line style is the
   wide list box on the left of the Borders toolbar. Click the
   down arrow to the right of the list box to see the line style
   options available.

4. Choose a border type (top, bottom, outside, and so on).
   Word immediately applies the border to the selection. You
   can choose more than one border type — top and bottom,
   for example.

5. Choose a shading pattern from the shading box if you want
   to add shading inside the border. The shading pattern box
   is the wide list box at the right end of the Borders toolbar.
   Click the down arrow to the right of the list box to see the
   shading pattern options available.

# Using the Paragraph Borders and Shading dialog box

The dialog box is slightly more complicated to use than the
Borders toolbar, but it offers several minor advantages not found
in the toolbar. You can specify both a shadowed border (which is
different than filling a border with shading) and how much space
to leave between the border and the text. You can also see a
preview of any shading you apply.

1. Select the element you want to have a border.

2. Choose Format⇨Borders and Shading to open the Paragraph Border and Shading dialog box.

3. Click the <u>B</u>orders tab to add borders.

4. Choose the Sh<u>a</u>dow option under Presets if you want a shadowed border. Otherwise, choose Bo<u>x</u>.

5. Choose a line St<u>y</u>le under Line. The Border area reflects your choice.

6. Adjust the numbers in the <u>F</u>rom Text box under Border to increase or decrease the distance from the border. Clicking the up arrow increases the distance. The Border area reflects any changes you make here.

7. Click the <u>S</u>hading tab and choose a shading pattern to add shading. The Preview box shows a sample of your choice.

8. Choose contrasting colors in the <u>F</u>oreground and B<u>a</u>ck-ground boxes if you want to add color shading; then scroll through the shading patterns to see the options available. (Remember that if you don't have a color printer, you cannot print the colors.)

9. Click OK to close the dialog box.

## More stuff

Don't be confused by the terms Foreground and Background colors. You must have at least two colors to provide contrast, so these terms simply identify the colors.

Also, don't be confused by the difference between shading and shadowed. Shading means filling the bordered area with a shaded pattern. Shadowed means giving the borders themselves a shadowed, three-dimensional look.

See *Word For Windows 6 For Dummies* for more on borders and shading.

## Bullets and Numbering

You can use bullets and numbers to number and emphasize lists and paragraphs, and you can use any symbol to represent a bullet, depending on the fonts you have installed. For routine tasks, using the Bullets or Numbering button on the Formatting toolbar sufficiently meets your needs. To customize your bullets and numbering, open the Bullets and Numbering dialog box.

## Inserting bullets or numbers

To insert bullets or numbers as you type, just click the Bullets or Numbering button on the Formatting toolbar. The button stays "on" until you click it again — as long as it's on a bullet or number appears in your text each time you press Return.

To insert bullets or numbers in paragraphs you have already entered, select the paragraphs and then click the appropriate button. Each paragraph you selected then appears with a bullet or number.

## Removing bullets and numbers

To remove existing bullets and numbers, select the paragraphs that contain the bullets or numbers you want to remove and then click the appropriate button (regular or numbered bullets) on the Formatting toolbar. This tactic only works on bullets and numbers that you originally inserted by using Word's Bullets and Numbering feature. In any other case, just select the bullets or numbers and press Delete.

## Modifying bullets

Word bullets are normally round dots, but you can use any symbol for a bullet that you want to create. You can select the symbols from the fonts that are installed on your computer, so if you have a lot of fonts you'll have a lot of symbols.

1. Choose Format⇨Bullets and Numbering to open the Bullets and Numbering dialog box.

2. Choose the <u>B</u>ulleted tab. At this point, you can choose any of the bullets that Word offers you and click OK to insert them immediately. To modify the bullets, continue to step 3.

3. Click the <u>M</u>odify button to open the Modify Bulleted List dialog box.

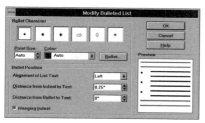

4. If the bullet you want appears in any of the six boxes under Bullet Character, click that box. If not, see step 6.

5. Adjust the size and color of the bullet in the <u>P</u>oint Size and <u>C</u>olor boxes.

6. To select a new bullet character, first select one of the six boxes to store the new symbol; then click the <u>B</u>ullet button to open the Symbol dialog box.

7. Select a symbol from this box. Click the down arrow to the right of the Symbols <u>F</u>rom box at the top of the dialog box to display a list of installed fonts. (Try Zapf Dingbats or Wingdings for interesting symbols, if you have these fonts installed.)

8. When you select a symbol, click OK to insert the symbol in the Bullet Character box you selected.

9. To adjust the position of the bullets in relation to the text, adjust the settings under Bullet Position. The Preview box reflects any adjustments you make.

10. Click OK to accept the modifications and close the dialog box.

## *Modifying numbered lists*

1. Choose F<u>o</u>rmat⇨Bullets and <u>N</u>umbering to open the Bullets and Numbering dialog box.

2. Select the <u>N</u>umbered tab. Once again, at this point you can choose any of the Numbered samples that Word offers and click OK to insert them immediately. To modify the numbers, continue to step 3.

3. Click the <u>M</u>odify button to open the Modify Numbered List dialog box.

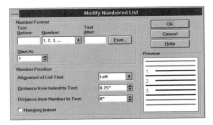

4. In the Number Format section, you can select a specific number format.

5. You can also choose to use text before and after the numbers in the numbered list. For example, if you want each paragraph to be numbered Item 1, Item 2, Item 3, and so on, type **Item** in the Text <u>B</u>efore box.

6. To change the font, click the <u>F</u>ont button.

7. To begin the numbered list at a number other than 1, enter that number in the <u>S</u>tart At box.

8. To adjust the position of the numbers in relation to the text, adjust the settings in the Number Position section. The Preview box reflects all adjustments.

9. Click OK to accept the modifications and close the dialog box.

## *Multilevel numbers*

This feature lets you insert numbers (or letters) unique to each level of multilevel paragraphs. Multilevel paragraphs are most commonly found in contracts and other legal documents that have subparagraphs.

The drawback to this feature is that it is not interactive — you cannot turn it on and have it insert the correct style of number for a particular paragraph. Instead, you must type all the paragraphs first, being careful to press Tab the correct number of times for each subparagraph. Then select all the paragraphs that need multilevel numbering and insert the numbers from the Bullets and Numbering dialog box. Word determines which paragraph gets which type of number based on how many tab characters precede the paragraph. Not very elegant, but it does work if you are meticulous about your subparagraph arrangement.

## *More stuff*

A quick way to tell if the numbers or bullets in a document were inserted (by using this feature) or typed into a document is to try to select one of them. If you cannot highlight the number of bullet, you know it was inserted using Word's Bullets and

Numbering feature. If you can successfully select one of them, they were typed as normal text.

To quickly open the Bullets and Numbering dialog box, click the right mouse button once; then select Bullets and Numbering from the shortcut menu.

## Canceling

Cancels a command, a selection, or printing.

- To cancel a command, press Esc.

- To cancel a selection (or deselect, if you prefer), click somewhere outside the selection or press an arrow key.

- To cancel a print job when Print Manager is disabled, press Esc. To cancel a print job when Print Manager is running, double-click the printer icon in the status bar or click the File menu and select Stop Printing.

See **Printing** for more on this topic.

## Captions

Adds captions to tables, pictures, and equations. You can manually add a caption or specify that Word automatically add captions to certain objects. Word keeps track of caption numbering for you.

## Inserting a caption manually

When you insert a caption, Word automatically numbers it for you. You can choose any of Word's numbering formats for the numbers in your captions.

1. Select the object that needs a caption.

2. Choose Insert⇨Caption to open the Caption dialog box.

3. Note Word's suggested caption in the Caption box. You can accept it, use a different caption, or create a new one.

4. To use a different caption, click the down arrow to the right of the Label box to display the available captions and then select the one you want.

5. To create an entirely new caption, click the New Label button to open the New Label dialog box. Type the new caption and click OK. Word automatically inserts the number for you.

6. If you want the caption to appear above the selected object, click the Position box and choose Above Selected Item.

7. To change the numbering format for the captions, click the Numbering button to open the Caption Numbering dialog box. In this dialog box, you can select a different numbering format, and you can include the chapter number in the captions if you wish. Click OK to return to the Caption dialog box.

8. Click OK to insert the caption.

## Automatic Captioning

You can specify that Word automatically insert a caption when you insert a picture from selected applications.

1. Choose Insert⇨Caption to open the Caption dialog box.

2. Click the AutoCaption button to open the AutoCaption dialog box.

3. Select the applications you use to insert pictures you want automatically captioned. You can select as many as you like.

4. You can set different options for each application. If you want to add a new caption to the default list, click the New Label button to open the New Label dialog box and type the caption. The label you type will be added to the list.

5. Click the Numbering button to open the Caption Numbering dialog box if you want to select a different numbering format or include the chapter number in the caption.

6. When you click OK in the AutoCaption dialog box, Word will insert a new caption automatically for objects you insert from the applications you selected.

# More stuff

Word actually uses *Sequence fields* when inserting a caption. This is how Word can correctly keep track of caption numbering. So, for example, if you insert a picture before an existing captioned picture, Word will automatically adjust the caption numbers so they are correct. Unfortunately, however, Word does not automatically update the caption numbering when you delete a captioned picture. Instead, you need to select the entire document (Edit⇨Select All) and press F9, which is the keystroke that instructs Word to update fields. This operation causes Word to resequence all the Sequence fields, thereby resulting in your captions being correctly numbered.

If you use Word's caption feature it is easy to create a table of figures or illustrations. See **Table of Figures** for more on this feature.

## Centering

Centering in Word is part of alignment formatting, which itself is part of paragraph formatting.

See **Alignment** for more on centering. For centering tables, see **Tables**.

### For keyboard kut-ups

Select the text or other item you want to center and press

### For mouse maniacs

Select the text or other item you want centered and click the Center button on the Formatting toolbar.

## Change Case

Lets you change the case of selected text according to different criteria. If, for example, you had typed a bunch of text while you inadvertently had Caps Lock turned on, you can select that text and toggle it so Word changes uppercase to lower and vice versa. Or you can select a sentence and have Word apply Sentence Case. A nifty feature.

## For keyboard kut-ups

To toggle among all uppercase, all lowercase, and first letter capitalized, select the text and press

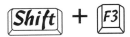

## Changing case

1. Select the text.

2. Choose Format⇨Change Case to open the Change Case dialog box.

3. Select the option you want. (Note that the options are themselves formatted in accordance with what they do.) The options available are:

   • Sentence case - capitalizes the first letter of the first word in a sentence

   • lowercase - makes all selected characters lowercase

   • UPPERCASE - makes all selected characters uppercase

   • Title Case - capitalizes first letter of each selected word

   • tOGGLE cASE - reverses case of all selected characters

4. Click OK.

## More stuff

One common method of selecting a sentence is to press Ctrl and click anywhere in the sentence. Word selects the sentence by searching for a period, so if the sentence contains an abbreviation that itself has a period (Mr., Ms., and so on), the selection will stop there. Be careful to select the entire sentence in such cases.

### Closing

Closes open files. Because Word for Windows allows you to have multiple open files, opening a file does not automatically close a previously opened file. You must use a separate action to close a file. Also, whenever you close an open file, you have to decide if you want to save any changes.

## For keyboard kut-ups

To close the active file, press

## Closing your files

1. Choose File⇨Close. If you've made changes to the file you want to close, Word prompts you to save the changes. (If the file hasn't been saved at least once before, you will have to give the file a name and specify a drive and directory for the file. See **Saving Files** for more on this operation.)

2. If you want to save the changes to the file, click Yes; otherwise click No.

## Closing Word

You can close Word from the File menu also. To do this, select File⇨Exit. If you have any unsaved files open, Word prompts you to save changes to those files first.

## More stuff

You can close all the open files at one time by pressing Shift while you click File. When you press Shift, the Close command becomes Close All. Word prompts you to save changes for each file that you have changed without saving.

## Columns

Creates newspaper-style columns (sometimes referred to as *snaking columns*) of text.

Don't confuse snaking columns with table columns. Table columns usually consist of numbers, but they can also contain text. Table column are handled quite differently from snaking columns and are covered under **Tables**. Also, snaking columns are related to *sections* in Word. If your document has varying numbers of columns, each set of columns must be in its own section. For more on this topic, see **Sections**.

## For mouse maniacs

If you want to change the number of columns in part of a document, select the text you want to change first. Click the Columns button on the Standard toolbar and drag to select the number of columns. Word will automatically insert the section breaks for you before and after the selected text. If you want an existing section of your document to have columns, make sure that the insertion point is somewhere in that section before you click the Columns button.

## Creating multiple columns

1. Choose <u>V</u>iew⇨<u>P</u>age Layout to be sure you are in page layout view.

2. Choose F<u>o</u>rmat⇨<u>C</u>olumns to open the Columns dialog box.

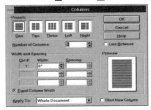

3. Make your selections and click OK.

## More stuff

 Remember that you can't see newspaper-style columns properly unless you're in page layout view or print preview. Normal view can display only a single column at a time.

 The total widths of each column and the spacing between columns must equal the amount of text space between your margins. Word keeps track of this for you (fortunately!). That's why, when you change the size of one column or the spacing between columns, Word adjusts all the other values automatically. If you want to increase the overall text space, you need to decrease your margin settings.

 You can easily create a headline that spans your columns. Just type the headline above the left column and press Enter to be sure that the headline is in its own paragraph. Then select the headline and format it as a single column. Finally, center the headline and format it with the font and font size you think appropriate.

 For more on this topic, see *Word For Windows 6 For Dummies*.

### Comparing Document Versions

Compares two versions of a document and allows you to accept or reject changes. The two versions must either have different filenames or be in different directories.

# Comparing versions

Begin this procedure by opening one of the two documents you want to compare and then follow the steps below.

1. Choose Tools⇨Revisions to open the Revisions dialog box.

2. Click the Compare Versions button to open the Compare Versions dialog box — really nothing more than the File Open dialog box — so that you can locate the other version of the file. When you locate the other file, click OK. Word compares the files internally and displays the edited file with revision marks that indicate new, deleted, and revised text.

3. Choose Tools⇨Revisions to accept or reject the revisions.

## More stuff

 Comparing versions of a document is actually part of a larger procedure called Revisions, which you can use to track changes with revision marks as you work in a document. For more on this topic see **Revisions**.

# Copying

Copies text and graphic objects to any Word document or any other Windows application. You can also copy various elements of Word (bookmarks, macros, styles, and so on) from one document or template to another.

## For keyboard kut-ups

To copy text or graphics, first select what you want to copy and then press

$$\boxed{Ctrl} + \boxed{C}$$

or

$$\boxed{Ctrl} + \boxed{Ins}$$

## For mouse maniacs

Select what you want to copy; then click the Copy button on the Standard toolbar.

## More stuff

 Copying something in Word (or any Windows application, for that matter) means placing it on the Clipboard. The Clipboard is a temporary storage area that Windows uses for items you cut or copy. When something is on the Clipboard, you can paste it into any Word document (or any Windows application, for that matter). The stuff that's on the Clipboard stays there until you cut or copy something else, so you can paste it as often as necessary.

Cutting and copying are similar operations. The only difference is that copying leaves the original selection in place and cutting removes the selection from its original location. In either case, the selection is placed on the Clipboard and remains there until you cut or copy something else.

Cutting, copying and pasting are really three parts of the same operation. For more on this, see **Cutting** and **Pasting**.

## Counting Words in Your Document

Lets you count the words, characters, paragraphs, and lines in a document or a selection.

## *Counting words and other stuff in your document*

Choose Tools⇨Word Count to open the Word Count dialog box.

The dialog box displays the number of words, characters, paragraphs, and lines in the document or selected portion of the document. You can enable the option to include footnotes and endnotes in the count.

## *Cross-Referencing*

Creates automatic cross-references, such as "See Chart 3 on page 12" to other parts of your document. You can update changes in the cross-reference automatically if the pages or the item number changes.

## *Creating cross-references*

1. Type the text that introduces the cross-reference (for example, "For more on this topic, see... ").

2. Choose Insert⇨Cross-reference to open the Cross-reference dialog box.

3. In the Reference Type box, select the type of cross-reference you want to create. The choice you make here determines what appears in the next two boxes.

4. In the Insert Reference To box, select what you want Word to insert in your document (for example, a heading title or a page number).

5. In the For Which box, select the specific item you want to cross-reference. If you want to refer to a figure and the document has a number of figures, select the specific figure here.

6. Click the Insert button to insert the cross-reference. The dialog box stays open so that you can continue creating cross-references.

7. Click the Close button to end the operation.

## Updating cross-references

Because Word uses fields to create cross-references, you can quickly update all the cross-references in the document by selecting the entire document and pressing F9. The F9 key updates all selected fields.

## More stuff

If you notice a strange code in braces where your cross-references should be, what you are seeing is a Word field code. Remember that this is how Word keeps track of all the cross-references in your document. To turn off the code, select it and press Alt+F9. This keystroke toggles field codes off and on. To turn off all field codes in your document at once, choose Tools⇨Options and click the View tab to be sure that Field Codes is disabled.

Cross-references are related to captions and bookmarks in that you can use these features to keep track of each other and to move around the document quickly. See **Bookmarks** and **Captions** for more on these topics. Also, refer to **Fields** for more on using field codes in Word.

## Databases

Inserts database information from database applications. You can also retrieve database information from another Word document, Microsoft Access and Excel, and any database application that has an ODBC (Open DataBase Connectivity) driver installed. You may be pleased to know that Word automatically installs ODBC drivers for Access, Paradox, Microsoft FoxPro, dBASE, and any application that has a file converter installed in Word — which just means that you can extract database information from these sources without worrying about conversion problems.

### *For mouse maniacs*

Display the Database toolbar and click the Insert Database button. With the Database toolbar, you can also insert, delete, and sort records, among other things.

### *Inserting a database from another application*

1. Position the insertion point where you want to insert the database.

2. Choose Insert⇨Database or click the Insert Database button on the Database toolbar to display the Database dialog box.

3. Click the Get Data button to open the Open Data Source dialog box. This dialog box looks and functions very much like the File Open dialog box.

4. Select the drive and directory that contain the database.

5. Click the Confirm Conversions option box if you want to be prompted before Word converts the database.

6. Select the file and click OK to return to the Database dialog box.

7. If you want to apply automatic formatting to the database, click the Table AutoFormat button. After you apply the format, click OK to return to the Database dialog box.

8. Click the Insert Data button to display the Insert Data dialog box. In this dialog box, you can select a range of records for the entire database to insert.

9. If you want to link the database file to the source application, click the Insert Data As Field button. When you enable this field, any changes made to the original database will also modify the database you insert in Word.

10. Click OK to insert the database as a Word table.

## Specifying which records to insert

You can specify which records you want to insert, based on the content of the records. This operation is called *querying*. You may want to insert a database of companies you do business with but only those companies that have annual gross earnings of more than $100,000. Or you can specify that only companies from certain states be included in the database. Of course, the information you seek has to be in the database in the first place.

1. Follow the preceding steps 1 through 6. (If you want Word to AutoFormat your table, include step 7.)

2. Click the Query Options button to open the Query Options dialog box. Click the Filter Records tab.

3. You can specify multiple fields and conditions. Click the first Field box to see a list of fields in the database and select the field you want to base the criteria on. (If you want to select companies with gross earnings of $100,000 or more, for example, select the field that contains earnings.)

4. Click the Comparison box to see a list of comparison factors. Select the comparison factor you want to use. (To follow the example in step 3, select Greater Than or Equal.)

5. Type the comparison value in the Compare To box. (Again, to follow the example in step 3, type $100,000. In steps 3 through 5 you specify that Word inserts records only on companies with annual gross earnings of $100,000 or more.)

6. If you want to add more conditions, move to the next line and select And or Or to specify the next condition.

7. Click OK when you finish specifying your conditions.

## More stuff

There is a fundamental difference between using *And* and *Or* (see preceding step 6). Using *And* might seem sensible to you, but it won't seem sensible to Word if you specify *And* when you add a new query (condition). When you use *And*, Word selects only records that meet *both* conditions, not *either* condition. So if you specify on the first line that you want records for companies in ZIP code 12345, then use *And* for the second line and specify ZIP code 23456, Word searches for records that contain both codes. After all, you did say *And*. Because no records contain more then one ZIP code, no records are selected. You have to think like a computer here!

There are a number of other things you can do when you insert a database: You can click the Sort Records tab or the Select Fields tab in the Query Options dialog box. The Sort Records option lets you sort the records according to specified criteria, and the Select Fields option lets you insert selected fields rather than the entire record.

For more on this topic, refer to *Word For Windows 6 For Dummies.*

## Date and Time

Inserts the date and the time in a specified format, either as text or as a field. You can enter the date, the time, or both in any of the formats included in Word. If you enter the date or time as a field, Word updates it each time you open the file. If you don't enter the date or time as a field, whatever date or time you enter originally will not change unless you edit it.

## For keyboard kut-ups

To insert the date as a field, press

$$\boxed{Alt} + \boxed{Shift} + \boxed{D}$$

To insert the time as a field, press

$$\boxed{Alt} + \boxed{Shift} + \boxed{T}$$

## Inserting the date and time

Choose Insert⇨Date and Time to open the Date and Time dialog box. Choose the format you want to use. If you want to insert the date or time as a field so that Word updates them each time you open the document, enable the Insert As Field box.

# Deleting

Deletes selected items. Generally in Word, all you need do is to select whatever it is you want to delete, then press Delete — but there are several other methods you can use as well.

## For keyboard kut-ups

To delete a character at a time without moving the insertion point, press

**Del**

To delete a word at a time without moving the insertion point, press

**Ctrl** + **Del**

To delete a character at a time while moving the insertion point backwards, press

**Backspace**

To delete a word at a time while moving the insertion point backwards, press

**Backspace** + **Ctrl**

## For mouse maniacs

Use the mouse to select any amount of text, a manually inserted page break, a section break, or a graphic; then press Delete.

## More stuff

 You can delete some items, such as bookmarks, frames, shading, AutoText and AutoCorrect entries, by using dialog boxes.

Deleting some elements can be a little tricky. For example, you can't delete a footnote or an annotation by selecting it and pressing Delete. You'll just get an error message stating that this isn't a valid action. Instead you have to delete the reference mark in the text.

## Drag and Drop

Drags selected text or other item to a new location and drops it there. In Word 6, you can select any part of your document and drag it to a new location — even a different file — and drop it there. Word 6 also lets you drag a selection from one document to another, provided that both documents are open and visible on-screen.

## Dragging and Dropping from one document to another

1. Be sure that both documents are open. You need to display both documents on-screen, so close or minimize any other open documents in Word.

2. Choose Window⇨Arrange All to arrange both documents on-screen horizontally.

3. Select the text or graphic you want to drag. After you make the selection, release the mouse button.

4. Move the mouse pointer inside the selection until it changes to an arrow pointing up and left. Then click and drag the selection across the borders into the other document window.

5. Release the mouse button to drop the text in its new location.

## More stuff

 If you try to use the drag and drop technique and it doesn't work, you need to turn it on. Choose Tools⇨Options, click the Edit tab, and enable the Drag and Drop Text Editing option.

 If you want to copy a selection from one document to another, follow the preceding steps with one change: press and hold Ctrl before you start step 4.

## Drawing in Word

Gives you access to the Drawing toolbar so that you can draw various graphic objects without leaving Word. This toolbar lets you draw lines, circles, ovals, rectangles, squares, polygons, and callouts. You can also enter text in the enclosed objects you draw. Word offers a variety of options for drawing lines, and you can fill enclosed drawing objects with colors and patterns. This capability offers a handy method of drawing organizational charts, flow charts, and other line drawings.

When you use any of the drawing buttons, Word prompts you to switch to Page Layout view, where you can create your drawing.

## Creating a drawing

1. Click the Drawing button on the Standard toolbar to display the Drawing toolbar.

2. Click any of the drawing buttons and then drag to create an object. Use the first five buttons on the toolbar to draw lines, squares/rectangles, circles/ovals, arcs, and freeform shapes. The sixth button is the Text Box button, and the seventh button is the Callout button. Use the remainder of the buttons to work with objects already created.

## More stuff

You can do so many things with Word's drawing tools that covering all of them in this Quick Reference is impossible. I advise you to experiment with this feature. Here are some tips for you.

- Creating a drawing and creating a picture in Word are two different things. You create a drawing by clicking one of the drawing buttons and working in Page Layout view. You create a picture by first clicking the Create Picture button to open Word's Picture screen. There are two differences between creating a picture and a drawing: Format⇨Picture is available for cropping and scaling your picture only if you use the Create Picture button, and you can see a picture but not a drawing in Normal view.

- You can *constrain* the drawing tools by using the Shift and Ctrl keys as you drag. For example, choosing the Rectangle button and pressing Shift as you drag creates a square rather than a rectangle. Pressing Ctrl draws the rectangle from the center of the graphic outward. You can also press Ctrl and Shift together. This is true of all enclosed objects you draw.

- Double-click a drawing tool to keep that tool in effect until you choose another button or do anything else other than drag.

See *Word For Windows 6 For Dummies* for more on this topic.

## Drop Caps

Drop Caps

Formats the first letter of a paragraph as a large capital letter that occupies two or more lines of text in the paragraph. Word lets you apply drop cap formatting to several letters or the entire first word of a paragraph. Drop cap formatting is used in desktop publishing to create a distinctive visual effect for your text.

## *Inserting a drop cap*

1. Position the insertion point anywhere in the paragraph that gets the drop cap. If you want to apply drop cap formatting to several letters or the first word of the paragraph, select the letters or the word.

2. Choose Format⇨Drop Cap to open the Drop Cap dialog box.

3. Choose either Dropped or In Margin. In Margin means the text will not wrap around the dropped cap.

4. To choose a different font, click the down arrow to the right of the Font list box.

5. In the Lines to Drop control, specify the number of lines you want the dropped cap to occupy in the paragraph. For example, if the paragraph consists of six lines and you want the drop cap to occupy the first four lines, note that here.

6. In the Distance from Text control, specify the distance you want the text to be from the drop cap.

7. Click OK to apply drop cap formatting. If you are not in Page Layout view, Word prompts you to switch to that view. Word applies drop cap formatting even if you do not switch to Page Layout view; however, the drop cap appears above the paragraph if you don't switch.

## More stuff

 When you apply drop cap formatting to a paragraph, the number of lines in the paragraph should increase because of the amount of space the drop cap takes.

## Endnotes

Inserts endnote reference marks in the text and endnotes at the end of a section or document. There's not much difference between endnotes and footnotes. The major difference is that footnotes appear directly below the text or at the bottom of the page, whereas endnotes appear at the end of the section or document. The default formatting for footnote and endnotes is different as well, but you can change the formatting. Endnotes and footnotes consist of the reference mark in the text (a number or symbol) and the actual endnote or footnote.

Word automatically renumbers endnotes and when you insert or delete one. For example, if you have three endnotes in your document and insert a new endnote between the first and second one, Word renumbers all the endnotes correctly and adjusts their position at the end of the section or document. This feature is also works if you drag an existing endnote reference mark to a new location in the document.

## For keyboard kut-ups

To insert an endnote and open the Endnote pane, press

$$\boxed{Alt} + \boxed{Ctrl} + \boxed{E}$$

## Inserting an endnote or footnote

1. Position the insertion pointer where you want the reference mark to appear in the text.

2. Choose Insert⇨Footnote to open the Footnote and Endnote dialog box.

3. Choose either Footnote or Endnote. Word inserts the reference mark and switches you to the footnote or endnote. If you are in Normal view, Word opens the Footnote or Endnote pane; if you are in Page Layout view, Word switches you to the actual footnote or endnote.

4. Type the footnote or endnote.

5. Click Close to return to your document.

## Viewing endnotes and footnotes

You can see your footnotes and endnotes in either Print Preview or Page Layout view. In Normal view, choose View⇨Footnotes to open the Endnote/Footnote pane. The View Footnote command is not available unless you have at least one endnote or footnote in your document.

## Deleting an endnote or footnote

To delete either an endnote or a footnote, you must select and delete the reference mark in the text (see **Annotations**). If you select the footnote or endnote itself and try to delete it, Word displays an error message. You can select text in an endnote or footnote to modify or delete it, however.

## More stuff

Word's Endnote and Footnote feature is quite comprehensive. For more on this topic, see *Word For Windows 6 For Dummies.*

## Envelopes

Creates and prints an envelope. You can also store the envelope information in a separate section in the document to print later.

## For mouse maniacs

Click the Create Envelope button on the Word 2.0 toolbar (not displayed by default).

## Creating and printing an envelope

1. If there is more than one address in the document, or if Word can't seem to correctly identify the address, select the delivery address in your document.

2. Choose Tools⇨Envelopes and Labels to open the Envelopes and Labels dialog box.

3. Click the Envelopes tab.

4. The Delivery Address box displays the address you selected in step 1. You can change all or any part of it by typing directly in the box.

5. Type an address in the Return Address box or accept the default. (Word takes the return address information from User Info.) If you don't want to print a return address on the envelope, click the Omit box.

6. To choose an envelope size, change the fonts for the mailing and return addresses, or specify other options, click the Options button.

7. To print the envelope, click the Print button.

8. To add the envelope to the document, click the Add to Document button. Word creates a new section at the beginning of the document and adds the envelope to the section. The page is set to zero.

9. To modify an existing envelope already attached to the document, click the Change Document button. (This button is available only if you previously added an envelope to the document.)

## *More stuff*

If you want to change the default return address that Word uses, choose Tools⇨Options and click the User Info tab. Type the new default address in the Mailing Address box.

This procedure is for single envelopes only. See **Mail Merges** for information about sending multiple letters.

## *Equation Editor*

Lets you create complex equations and insert them into your document. In Word 6 you can create equations in place in your document because the Equation Editor tools and menu bar are available inside Word.

## Creating equations

1. Choose Insert⇨Object to open the Object dialog box.

2. Click the Create New tab.

3. Double-click Microsoft Equation 2.0. This displays the Equation toolbar and menu bar, and you can begin creating the equation. If previous versions of Word for Windows were installed on your computer, both Microsoft Equation 1.0 and 2.0 are listed; otherwise, only Microsoft Equation 2.0 is listed.

4. Use the Equation Editor toolbar to insert the various symbols for your equation. For help with step-by-step instructions, press F1.

5. When you have finished, click in any part of your Word document to close the Equation Editor toolbar and change the menus back to the Word menus.

## Editing equations

Because equations created in the Equation Editor are embedded objects, all you need to do to edit such an equation is to double-click it.

## More stuff

The Equation Editor may seem complex and confusing at first, but it is actually quite easy to use. Use the step-by-step instructions to guide you through the various parts of the toolbar. Also, for more information on using the Equation Editor, see *Word For Windows 6 For Dummies.*

Equation Editor is one of three supplementary applications to help you add special text effects, equations, and charts to documents. The other two are WordArt and MS Graph. These applications all use object linking and embedding (OLE). For more on these topics, see **WordArt, Graph,** and **OLE.**

---

**Exit**

Closes Word. This command has no other use.

## For keyboard kut-ups

To close Word, press

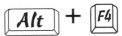

or

$$\boxed{Alt} + \boxed{F}$$

then press

$$\boxed{X}$$

## Closing Word

To close Word, choose File➪Exit. If you have any unsaved files open, Word prompts you to save each file.

## Fields

Allow you to insert and update information in a document. For example, if you insert a page number field in your document, Word automatically updates the page numbers as you modify the document. Or if you insert a date field, Word automatically updates the date each time you save the document.

Field codes consist of the field braces, which look just like braces you type but are not (Word does not recognize typed braces as field codes); the field code itself; and switches that modify the way the field works. Word's default is to display the information the field represents, but you can view the field codes instead.

Word has over 60 field types that you can use in your documents. Some fields can be modified to perform slightly different tasks by adding one or more switches. Field categories in Word include: Date and Time, Document Automation, Document Information, Equations and Formulas, Indexes and Tables, Links and References, Mail Merge, Numbering, User Information.

## For keyboard kut-ups

To insert a date field, press

$$\boxed{Alt} + \boxed{Shift} + \boxed{D}$$

To insert a page number field, press

$$\boxed{Alt} + \boxed{Shift} + \boxed{P}$$

To insert a time field, press

$$\boxed{Alt} + \boxed{Shift} + \boxed{T}$$

To update a selected field, press

To insert the field braces and position the insertion point inside the braces, press

## Inserting a field

1. Place the insertion point where you want to insert the field.
2. Choose Insert⇨Field to open the Field dialog box.

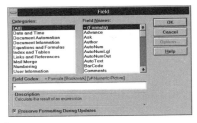

3. Choose the field category from the list in the Categories box.
4. Choose the actual field from the Field Names list box. A description of the field appears in the Description box.
5. To modify what the field does, click the Options button. This button is available only when you choose a field that can be modified. When you click the Options button, the Field Options dialog box is displayed, and Word lists any switches (modifiers) that the field can use. When you choose a switch, a description of what that switch does is displayed in the Description box.
6. To insert the field, click OK.

## Viewing field codes and results

Fields are codes that represent information. The information a field code represents is called the *field result* (Word's way of saying "this is the information that results from using this field"). You can see either the code or the result it represents. Word's default is to display the field result, but you can view the code instead. To view field codes in your document, choose Tools⇨Options, click the View tab, and enable Field Codes.

## Updating fields

To update a field, select it and press F9. If the information that the field represents has changed (that is, an index or table of contents), the most current information is displayed.

## More stuff

Fields are an important element of Word and cannot be covered comprehensively in this guide. For example, you can lock and unlock fields, unlink fields, and print field codes instead of field results. For more on using fields in Word, see *Word For Windows 6 For Dummies.*

## Files

Files are what you create when you save your documents. In Word, opening a file means you are retrieving an existing file. When you work with a file, you have to open it first. When you create a new file, you have to save it so that you can retrieve it later and work with it again. Because Word allows you to have more than one file open at a time, you have to manually close your files when you finish working with them. You can also save an open file as a separate file with a new name.

## For keyboard kut-ups

To save a file, press

$$Shift \quad + \quad F12$$

To save an existing file with a different name or in a different location, press

$$F12$$

To open a file, press

$$Ctrl \quad + \quad F12$$

## File menu options

To create a file, choose File⇨New to open the New dialog box, where you can choose the template you want to use for your new file. The default template is Normal.

To close an open file, choose File⇨Close. To close all open files, press Shift and choose File⇨Close All.

To open an existing file, choose File⇨Open to open the Open dialog box. You can change drives and directories here to choose the file or files you want to open.

To search for a file based on summary information or file content, choose File⇨Find File to open the Find File dialog box.

To save a file, choose File⇨Save. The first time you save a file, this command opens the Save As dialog box, where you can specify a drive and directory for the file and give it a name. After you name a file, choose File⇨Save to write any changes to the disk without opening a dialog box.

To save an existing file with a new name and/or to a different drive or directory, choose File⇨Save As. This command opens the Save As dialog box, where you can give the open file a new name and/or specify a new location for that file. When you use this option, Word closes the original file and stores it in its original drive and directory.

To save all open files, choose File⇨Save All. This command also saves macros and AutoText entries. Word prompts you separately for each item.

## More stuff

For more on saving files, see **Saving.** For more on opening files, see **Opening Files.**

Understanding how Word handles files is very important. For more on using files in Word, see *Word For Windows 6 For Dummies.*

## Find and Replace

Lets you search for and replace specific elements of your document. This command is very powerful and can save you quite a bit of time in many situations. Finding and replacing are actually two separate functions in Word. The Find dialog box lets you search for specific elements of your document. (However, you can click the Replace button in the Find dialog box to open the Replace dialog box.) The Replace dialog box includes the Find function but also allows you to change whatever it is you find, either globally or individually.

## For keyboard kut-ups

To open the Find dialog box, press

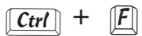

 After you specify what you want to find in the Find or Replace
dialog box, you can click the Find Next button in the dialog box to
move your search through the document; or you can click the
Cancel button to exit the dialog box and simply press Shift+F4 to
search for additional instances.

## Finding and Replacing in Word

1. Choose Edit⇨Replace to open the Replace dialog box.

*Note:* Most of the settings in the Find dialog box work just like the
Replace dialog box.

2. Type the text you want to find in the Find What box. Check
the Format button to choose Font, Paragraph, Language or
Style. Click the Special button to access a list of special
characters.

3. Type the text you want to insert in the Replace With box.
check the Format button to choose Font, Paragraph,
Language or Style. Click the Special button to access a list
of special characters.

4. To find each occurrence in order, click the Find Next button.

5. To replace a specific instance, click the Replace button.

6. To replace all instances at once, click the Replace All button.

## More stuff

 You can work in your document while the Find or Replace dialog
box is open. Just click in the document. To use the dialog box
again, click in the document to make it active.

 You can replace your selection with the contents of the Clipboard.
In this way, you can quickly insert a graphic that you use repeatedly throughout your document. For example, you can type
something like **XXX** where you want to insert the graphic. Later,

copy the graphic to the Clipboard. Then, in the Find What box, enter **XXX**. Move to the Replace With box, click the Special button, and choose Clipboard Contents. This procedure replaces each instance of XXX with the graphic you copied to the Clipboard.

See *Word For Windows 6 For Dummies* for more on finding and replacing in Word.

---

## Find File

Allows you to search for files based on summary information or file content. Summary information is information you can enter about a file in addition to its filename. You can also use Find File to print multiple documents without opening them; delete, copy, and sort documents; and preview documents. For most purposes, using Find File is perfectly safe, but you must be careful if you decide to delete files.

## Using File Find

1. Choose File⇔Find File to display the File Find dialog box. A list of files based on the previous search criteria appears in the Listed Files box. On your first search, the Search dialog box appears.

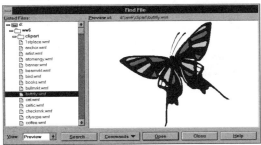

2. To see a preview of a listed file, choose the file and then choose Preview in the View box at the bottom. A preview of the chosen file appears in the Preview box. Use the scroll bar to the right of the previewed document to scroll through the document in the Preview box.

3. To see information about a file, select the file and then choose either File Info or Summary in the View box at the bottom.

4. To open the chosen file, click the Open button.

5. To close the File Find dialog box, click the Close button.

# Searching by filename and drive

When you first open the Find File dialog box, you see a list of files
based on the criteria you entered the previous time you used this
feature (unless it is the very first time you use the feature, in
which case the Search dialog box opens automatically). This is
fine if the list of files is the list you want. If, however, you want to
locate a file that isn't on the list, you need to conduct a search. If
you know the filename or even a part of the filename of the file
you want and the drive it is on, you can use the Search dialog box
to find your file.

1. Choose File⇨Find File to open the File Find dialog box.

2. Click the Search button to open the Search dialog box.

3. Enter the filename in the File Name box. You can also enter
   types of files using wildcard characters (**\*.txt, \*.doc,** and so
   on) in the box or click the down arrow to the right of the
   box to choose a type.

4. Enter the drive and directory you want to search in the
   Location box. You can enter multiple drives and directories
   by separating them with semicolons. To search
   subdirectories, click the Include Subdirectories option.

5. To start the search and return to the Find File dialog box,
   click OK. The Find File dialog box displays a list of files in
   the drives and directories you specified.

# Using the Advanced Search dialog box

If you don't know the drives or directories where the file or files
you want are located, you can specify additional search criteria,
such as summary information and file content. Such criteria are
known as *advanced searches*. Remember, though, that you cannot
search summary information about a file unless you save such
information. But you can always search for text within a file.

The Advanced Search dialog box has three tabs so that you can
enter different criteria for the search: Location, Summary, and
Timestamp.

1. Choose File⇨Find File to open the File Find dialog box.

2. Click the Search button to open the Search dialog box.

3. Click the Advanced Search button to open the Advanced Search dialog box.

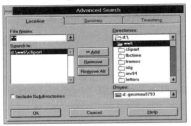

4. To browse through drives and directories, click the Location tab. Use the Directories and Drives boxes on the right side of the dialog box to scroll to the different drives and directories. To add a drive and directory, select it and click the <<Add button.

   If you inadvertently add a directory to the Search In box, choose it and click the Remove button, or click the Remove All button to clear the Search In box.

5. To search summary information (which must have been previously entered) or text contained in the file you are trying to locate, click the Summary tab. In the dialog box, enter the summary information you want Word to use for your search.

6. To narrow the search criteria by entering a range of dates a file was created or saved, click the Timestamp tab.

7. When you have chosen all the criteria you want, click OK to return to the Search dialog box.

8. Click OK in the Search dialog box to return to the Find File dialog box. Word displays all files that match the criteria you set.

## Saving search criteria

You can save a set of search criteria and give it a name. In this way, you can reuse that set of criteria any time you wish.

1. Choose File⇨Find File to display the File Find dialog box.

2. Click the Search button to open the Search dialog box.

3. Click the Advanced Search button to open the Advanced Search dialog box.

4. Choose the search criteria as previously outlined.

5. Click OK to return to the Search dialog box.

6. Click the <u>S</u>ave Search As button. This opens the Save Search As dialog box.

7. Enter a name for the search criteria and click OK.

## Using saved search criteria

To use a saved set of search criteria, follow steps 1 and 2 to open the Search dialog box. Click the down arrow to the right of this box to display all the saved searches and choose the search you want. All your saved searches appear in the Saved S<u>e</u>arches box. When you click the OK button, Word immediately begins a search based on the saved criteria.

## Using File Find to manage your files

The Find File feature in Word allows you to copy, open, print, and delete multiple files while still in Word. To do these things, you first need to find the files you want to manage and list them in the Find File dialog box. When the documents you want to manage are available in the Find File dialog box, you can work with them. You can also create directories using Find File.

1. Choose <u>F</u>ile⇨<u>F</u>ind File to display the File Find dialog box.

2. In the Find File dialog box, choose the files you want to use.

3. To choose multiple contiguous files, choose the first file, press the Shift key, and click the last file in the list. The two files you clicked on and all the files in between are selected. To choose multiple noncontiguous files, click the first file you want to choose, press Ctrl, and click additional files to choose them. To deselect a chosen file, press Ctrl and click the file.

4. To open the chosen files, click the Open button. To perform other tasks, click the <u>C</u>ommands button and choose the appropriate command.

## Creating a new directory using Find File

This task doesn't have anything to do with copying files, but it's a neat way to create directories.

1. Choose <u>F</u>ile⇨<u>F</u>ind File to display the File Find dialog box.

2. Click the <u>C</u>ommands button and choose <u>C</u>opy to open the Copy dialog box.

3. Click the New button to open the Create Directory dialog box.

4. Type the full path and new name of the directory you want to create and click OK to return to the Copy dialog box.

5. Click Close.

## More stuff

You can use the Advanced Search dialog box to search for a file based on a text string contained in the file. For example, if you have a printout of the file you need to find, you can enter a string of text in the <u>C</u>ontaining Text box. Word searches for that text string in any files it finds that meet the other criteria you set. You must be careful to enter text exactly as it appears in the file, including spacing and capitalization.

The more criteria you specify, the longer it takes to find your files. Also, if you specify incorrect criteria, you not only waste time, but you won't find your files. For example, if you specify a keyword but misspell it, Word cannot find the file. In most instances, specifying fewer criteria is better.

See **Summary Information** for more on this topic.

For more on using Find File, see *Word For Windows 6 For Dummies.*

## Font Formatting (formerly Character Formatting)

Formats selected text according to your specifications — bold, italic, underlined, and so on. The key to character formatting text in Word is that you must first select the text and then format it. If you select only part of a word, then only that part is formatted. Font, or character, formatting is a toggle: You apply and remove formatting by using the same commands.

## For keyboard kut-ups

For you keyboard fanatics, font formatting is easy, as illustrated in the following table:

| Format | Keystroke |
|---|---|
| Bold | Ctrl + B |
| Italics | Ctrl + 1 |
| Hidden text | Ctrl + Shift + H |
| Small caps | Ctrl + Shift + K |
| Underline entire selection | Ctrl + U |

| Underline word by word | Ctrl + Shift + W |
|---|---|
| Double underline | Ctrl + Shift + D |

## For mouse maniacs

The Formatting toolbar was designed for you mouse maniacs. It combines the most common character and paragraph formatting elements (and some other goodies), and, of course, you can modify it to suit yourself. The character formats on the Formatting toolbar let you change fonts and font sizes, as well as bold, italicize, and underline selected text. Simply select the text first and then click the appropriate button.

## Font dialog box

Choose Format Font to display the Font dialog box that contains all the possible font formatting available in Word. The two tabs in the Font dialog box are Font and Character Spacing.

## More stuff

The Spacing tab in the Font dialog box offers new options that may be unfamiliar. I created the following example by typing the line of text, selecting it, and formatting it as Times New Roman 14 bold. (Times New Roman is a TrueType font.) Next I selected the single capital letter at the beginning of the sentence (the *C*) and formatted it as 36 points with its Spacing Condensed by 8.5 points. Then, I selected the rest of the word (*ombining*) and formatted the Position as Raised by 7 points. Next, I selected the word (*font*) and formatted its Position as Lowered by 7 points. I lowered the position of the word *settings* by 14 points. (The word *unusual* is the only word in this paragraph on the baseline.) Finally, I centered the paragraph and put a border around it. Try it.

$$\text{C}\;\text{ombining}\quad \text{unusual}\;\text{font}\;\text{settings}$$

## Footnotes

Inserts footnote reference marks in the text and footnotes directly below the text or at the bottom of the page. Footnotes and Endnotes in Word are almost the same, except that endnotes appear at the end of a section or document, whereas footnotes appear at the bottom of the page or directly under the text.

## For keyboard kut-ups

To open the Footnote and Endnote dialog box, press

$$[Alt] + [Ctrl] + [F]$$

See **Endnotes** for more on this topic.

## Forms

Creates forms that can be completed in Word or printed and then completed. When creating a form to be completed by other users in Word, you should use a template that has some areas available for the user to fill-in and other areas protected from changes by the user. The areas where users make entries are form fields. The three form fields are text, check box, and drop-down list. After you create a protected-form template, users can create new forms that have the same protection as the template.

## Creating a form

1. Choose File⇨New to open the New dialog box.

2. Choose Template in the New section to create a new template.

3. Add the text and formatting to your form.

4. When you want to add a form field, Insert⇨Form Field to open the Form Field dialog box.

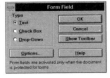

5. Choose the type of form field — Text, Check Box, or Drop Down — in the Type box.

6. Click the <u>O</u>ptions button to open the Options dialog box. A different Options dialog box opens for each type of form field, so the one you get in this step depends on what you choose in step 5.

7. Choose the options you want and click OK to close the Options dialog box.

8. When you add all the form fields, choose <u>T</u>ools⇨<u>P</u>rotect Document to open the Protect Document dialog box.

9. Choose <u>F</u>orms and add a <u>P</u>assword, if you like. If you add a password, only those who know the password can make changes to the template.

10. Save and close your new form template. Users can now create new forms based on the template you created. They can type only in the form fields that you used in the form.

## More stuff

You may find that using the Forms toolbar is easier and quicker. This toolbar allows you to insert any of the three types of form fields, use the Options dialog box for each of the form fields, insert a table and a frame, shade the form fields, and protect the document.

Creating forms in Word is not difficult once you get the hang of it. However, this topic is too large to be covered completely here. For more on this topic, see *Word For Windows 6 For Dummies.*

## Framing

Precisely positions objects anywhere on a page. The only items in a Word document that you cannot put into a frame are footnotes, endnotes, and annotations. After you insert a frame around an item, you can position that item anywhere on the page, either by dragging it or by entering precise values in the Frame dialog box. One minor drawback to framed items is that they do not appear correctly positioned when you are in Normal view, so you should work in Page Layout view when you work with frames.

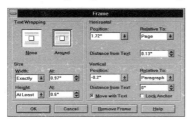

## *Inserting a frame*

When you insert a frame, Word automatically selects the frame so that you can work with it immediately. A selected frame has a cross-hatched border and eight black handles around the frame. You can use the handles to resize the framed object.

1. Switch to Page Layout view. If you don't switch to Page Layout view first, Word prompts you when you attempt to insert the frame.

2. Select the item you want to frame.

3. Choose Insert⇨Frame. Alternatively, click the Frame button. If you switched to Page Layout view, Word displays the cross-hatched border and the handles so you can work with the framed object immediately.

## *More stuff*

 See *Word For Windows 6 For Dummies* for more on framing.

## *GoTo*

Allows you to move quickly to a specified location in your document.

## *For keyboard kut-ups*

To open the GoTo dialog box, press

## *For mouse maniacs*

To open the GoTo dialog box, double-click the page number in the Status bar at the bottom of the Word window.

## *Using GoTo*

1. Choose Edit⇨Go To to open the GoTo dialog box.

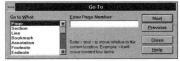

2. Select the element you want to go to from the list in the Go To What box.

3. Click Close or press Esc to close the GoTo dialog box.

## More stuff

You can click in your document and work while the GoTo dialog box is open. To use GoTo again, just click in the dialog box once to make it active.

You can scroll through your document quickly using the GoTo dialog box. Choose Page, Section, or Line in the Go To What box. To scroll forward to the next page, section, or line, click the Next button. To scroll back, click the Previous button. Because the dialog box remains open, you can scroll to wherever you want in your document.

---

## Grammar Checker

Checks sentences for grammar and other errors. You can specify what level of strictness Word uses to perform grammar checks. A grammar check in Word includes checking the spelling.

## Using the grammar checker

1. Choose Tools⇨Grammar to begin the check. Word displays the Grammar dialog box when it finds a sentence with questionable grammar or style.

2. Click the Change button to accept the suggested edit or change.

3. To edit the sentence, type your changes in the Sentence box.

4. To ignore the current rule for the rest of the grammar check, click the Ignore Rule button.

5. To ignore the particular suggestion, click the Ignore button.

6. To continue the grammar check, click the Next Sentence button.

7. To reverse the last grammar change, click the Undo Last button.

8. To see details about the current grammar rule, click the Explain button.

9. When the grammar check is complete, Word displays readability statistics in the Readability Statistics dialog box. Click OK to return to your document.

## Setting grammar options

You can open the Grammar Options dialog box either by clicking the Options button in the Grammar dialog box or by choosing Tools⇨Options and then choosing the Grammar tab.

## More stuff

Spell checking can be accomplished during a grammar check if you enable the Check Spelling option in the Grammar Options dialog box. For more on using Word's spell checker, see **Spelling Checker.**

## Graphics in Word

Allows you to add graphics to your documents. You can create graphic objects in other applications and paste, link, or embed them in your document. You can insert graphics using the Insert Picture command. You can also draw graphic objects using the Drawing toolbar or MS Draw (an add-in program). Depending on the approach you take to add the graphic to your file, you can use either the original application or Word's drawing tools to edit the graphic.

## Inserting a picture

1. Choose Insert⇨Picture to open the Insert Picture dialog box.

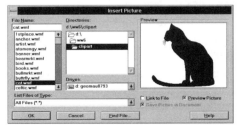

2. Choose the drive and directory where the graphics file is located.

3. Choose the file from the list in the File Name box.

4. Choose the type of graphic file you want to insert from the list in the List Files of Type box. To see all the graphics files in the drive and directory specified, choose All Files.

5. To see a preview of the chosen file, enable the Preview Picture option under the Preview box.

6. To link the file to its source application, enable the Link To File option under the Preview box.

## More stuff

When you create a graphic in another application, you can copy it to the Clipboard and then paste it into your Word document. This approach lets you link or embed the graphic. See **Linking** and **OLE** for more on linking and embedding.

Word provides a Drawing toolbar for you to create graphics of your own. See **Drawing in Word** for more on this topic.

Because Word is a graphically oriented word processing system, the topic of using graphics in Word is extensive. You can use a number of concepts and procedures, and there are variations on each procedure. For more on graphics and Word, see *Word For Windows 6 For Dummies*.

## Graphs

Use Microsoft Graph to insert graphs and charts into your Word document. A graph and a chart are really the same thing: They graphically represent numbers. You can use Excel or any Windows spreadsheet to create and insert charts in your Word document, but if you don't know how to use a spreadsheet or just want to create a simple chart, you can use Graph instead.

## Creating a chart in MS Graph

You can create a chart from an existing table in your Word document, or you can open MS Graph and add the numbers directly to create the chart.

1. If you have a table you want to use in a chart, select the table. Otherwise, go to step 2.

2. Click the Chart button on the Standard toolbar (or Insert⇨Object, click the Create New tab, and choose Microsoft Graph) to open the Microsoft Graph window.

3. If you selected a table in step 1, the graph automatically represents the numbers in the table. Otherwise, click in the datasheet window and add the numbers just as you would to a Word table or an Excel worksheet.

4. Choose the type of chart you want from the Gallery menu.

5. Choose any other options you want.

6. To insert the chart into your Word document, File➪Exit And Return.

## *More stuff*

To edit a chart you created in MS Graph, double-click in it. Because it is an embedded object, Graph opens for you to edit the chart.

Press F1 for help any time while you are working in Graph. This help provides you with information on the different options and gives you instructions on how to use Graph.

For more on using MS Graph and the other Word add-ins, see *Word For Windows 6 For Dummies.*

## *Headers and Footers*

Inserts text and graphics in the top and bottom margins in your document. Stuff in the top margin is a header, and stuff in the bottom margin is a footer. Headers and footers are section-specific, which means that you have to create a new section whenever you want to change a header or footer in your document. It also means that any change you make to a header or footer affects every header or footer in that section.

## *Creating a header or footer*

1. Choose View➪Header And Footer. Word opens the Header And Footer toolbar and switches to Header and Footer view. In this view you can see the headers and footers, but the document text is dimmed. The header and footer are enclosed in a dashed line that does not print.

2. To switch between headers and footers, click the Between Header And Footer button on the Header And Footer toolbar.

3. To suppress the document text, click the Show/Hide Document Text button. You'll probably find this view easier to use.

4. To move to the header or footer in the previous section, click the Show Previous button. To move to the header or footer in the next section, click the Show Next button.

5. To enter text, type the text with the dashed lines surrounding the header or footer area.

6. To enter page numbers, click the Page Number button.

7. To enter the current date, click the Date button. To enter the current time, click the Time button.

8. To return to the document, click the Close button or double-click anywhere in the body of the document.

## Creating a different header or footer for the first page

You can specify a different header or footer for the first page of a document. If the document has more than one section, you can specify a different header or footer for the first page of a section.

1. Choose View⇨Header And Footer. Word opens the Header And Footer toolbar and switches to Header and Footer view.

2. Click the Page Setup button on the Header And Footer toolbar to open the Page Setup dialog box.

3. Choose the Layout tab.

4. Enable the Different First Page option under Headers and Footers and click OK to return to the Header and Footer view.

5. To move to the first page header or footer of the document or section, click the Show Previous button. The header and footer boxes indicate First Page Header (or Footer).

6. Type the text you want on the first page. If you want the first page not to have a header or footer, just leave them blank. You can also leave one blank and enter text or graphics in the other.

7. To move to the header or footer for the rest of the section or document, click the Show Next button. Create the header or footer you want for the rest of the section or document. Of course, you must have a second page before Word lets you enter a "rest of section" header.

8. Click the Close button to return to your document or double-click anywhere in the body of the document.

## Creating different headers or footers for odd and even pages

Creating different headers or footers for odd and even pages is actually the same procedure as creating a different first page header, except that this option applies to odd and even pages. For example, you might want to align the headers and footers on the left for even pages and on the right for odd pages. You can combine this effect with the Different First Page effect. To create different headers for odd and even pages, follow the steps for creating a different header or footer for the first page with one exception. In step 4 you should enable the Different Odd and Even Page option instead of the Different First Page option. Or you can enable them both.

## Creating different headers or footers in the same document

When you first insert a header or footer, Word inserts it on every page of the document (unless you specify Different First Page). You can create an entirely different header or footer in any part of your document if you wish. Remember that different headers and footers require a section break. If your document already has the section breaks you need, you can skip steps 1 - 3.

1. Position the insertion point at the beginning of the page where you want the different header or footer.

2. Choose Insert⇨Break to open the Break dialog box.

3. Under Section Breaks, choose Next Page to replace the page break with a next page section break. (You must delete the page break separately if you inserted it manually.)

4. Choose View⇨Header And Footer. Word opens the Header And Footer toolbar and switches to Header and Footer view.

5. Click the Same As Previous button. This option disconnects the header and footer from the previous section. (Word copies existing headers and footers automatically to a new section, so your first step needs to be to disable the default header/footer before you can enter the new one.)

6. Delete the existing header or footer.

7. Create the header or footer you want. Word inserts the new header or footer in this section and all sections that follow this one. If you need to create new sections, close the Header and Footer view and repeat steps 1 - 3.

8. To return to your document, click the Close button or double-click anywhere in the body of the document.

## More stuff

You can insert a section break while you are in Header and Footer view. Be sure that the insertion point is on the page where you want the new header or footer before opening Header and Footer view. Then click the Page Setup button and choose the Layout

tab. Under Section Start choose New Page. In the Apply To box choose This Point Forward. Word inserts a section break at the beginning of that page, and you can go ahead and delete the existing header or footer and create your new one.

For more on headers and footers, see *Word For Windows 6 For Dummies.*

## Heading Numbering

Word has nine built-in heading styles that you can apply to headings in documents that contains lists, such as outlines and legal and technical documents. These heading styles are in addition to the Bullets and Numbering feature. When you apply one of the built-in heading styles, Word formats that heading according to the default definition of that heading style. You can, of course, change the definition of any heading style manually, but Word provides an automated method of quickly numbering such headings and applying indentation to subordinate headings throughout an entire document.

## Using heading numbering

The Heading Numbering feature can be applied only to headings that use Word's built-in heading styles.

1. Choose Format⇨Heading Numbering to open the Heading Numbering dialog box.

2. Choose one of the six thumbnail styles for your headings and click OK.

## Modifying heading numbering

You can modify any of the thumbnail styles that appear in the Heading Numbering dialog box in a variety of ways.

1. Choose Format⇨Heading Numbering to open the Heading Numbering dialog box.

2. Choose one of the six thumbnail styles and click the Modify button to open the Modify Heading Numbering dialog box.

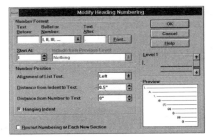

3. Choose the options you want.

4. Click OK to return to your document. Word applies the Heading Numbering options you chose.

## More stuff

 Word's built-in heading styles are useful in other ways as well. You can use them in Outline view to reorganize your document quickly, and Word uses them to create an automated table of contents. Familiarizing yourself with Word's numbering styles is definitely worth your while.

 For more on both Word's built-in numbering styles and number heading formatting, see *Word For Windows 6 For Dummies*.

# Help

You can get extensive help with almost anything in Word in a variety of ways. Word's Help feature is extensive and makes good use of *jumping*. Note that many words and phrases are formatted in green. These are jump terms. If you click such an item, Word jumps immediately to that topic. Some words and phrases are formatted in green text with a dotted underline. If you click one of these items, Word displays the meaning of the underlined word or phrase. Click again to close the meaning window.

## For keyboard kut-ups

Any time you want help, press

## For mouse maniacs

Click the Help button on the Standard toolbar to transform the pointer into a help tool. Word attaches a question mark to the pointer. You can point at any element and click to get help on that element. This includes menu items (but only the available commands on a menu). If you point at text and click, Word displays the paragraph and font formatting applied to that text.

## Using Help

There are many ways to use help in Word. This procedure is only one basic approach. Experiment! You'll learn much and come to appreciate the Help feature.

1. Choose Help⇨Contents to open the Help window. Word displays several basic help categories.

2. Click any category to jump to another help screen on that topic.

3. Note that the Word Help window has both menus and buttons.

4. Close the Help window as you would any other window.

## More stuff

To see interesting and valuable information about your system and the available system resources, choose Help⇨About Microsoft Word to open the About Microsoft Word dialog box. Click the System Info button at the bottom of this dialog box to open the Microsoft System Info window. Here you can choose different categories and see information about them, and you can print and save that information. You can also run certain Windows system applications from this dialog box.

For more on using Word's extensive help system and its demos, see *Word For Windows 6 For Dummies.*

## Hidden Text

Formats selected text as hidden text. Hidden text is a font attribute (that is, you format text as hidden in the same way that you format text as bold or italic). Word also automatically formats certain fields as hidden: table of contents entries, index entries, and annotations. You can use hidden text to leave yourself and others notes that won't print.

## For keyboard kut-ups

Select the text you want to format and press

## Formatting text as hidden

1. Select the text.

2. Choose Format⇨Font to open the Font dialog box; then click the Font tab.

3. Under Effects, enable the Hidden option.

## Displaying and hiding text

You can display hidden text by clicking on the Show/Hide button on the Formatting toolbar so that nonprinting characters (paragraph marks, tabs, and so on) are visible. When you click on the Show/Hide button to make nonprinting characters invisible, hidden text disappears from view but is still part of the document. To display hidden text without showing the other nonprinting characters, choose  Tool⇨Options and click the View tab. Enable the Hidden Text option under nonprinting characters.

## Printing hidden text

Even if you display hidden text in normal or page layout view, you cannot see it in print preview unless you choose to print it.

1. Choose File⇨Print to open the Print dialog box.

2. Click the Options button to open the Print Options dialog box.

3. Enable the Hidden Text option under Include With Document and click OK.

## More stuff

Printing and displaying hidden text may affect your document's pagination, depending on how much hidden text you have in the document. If you have a table of contents or an index in your document, be sure that you hide hidden text and specify that it not print, to keep your page references accurate.

# *Hyphenation*

Inserts hyphens when a word would otherwise wrap to the next line. Hyphenation can improve the appearance of a document, especially justified text.

## *Hyphenating automatically as you type*

1. Choose Tools⇨Hyphenation to open the Hyphenation dialog box.

2. Enable the Automatically Hyphenate Document option.

3. Enter the amount of space you want in the Hyphenation Zone. This space is an area Word uses to determine if a word should be hyphenated. The larger the space, the fewer hyphens. The smaller the space, the less ragged your document appears.

4. If you want to limit the number of consecutive lines that can be hyphenated, enter a number in the Limit Consecutive Hyphens To box.

5. Click OK to return to your document and begin hyphenating.

If you don't want some part of your document to be hyphenated, select that part of you document and Format⇨Paragraph; then click the Text Flow tab. Enable the Don't Hyphenate option.

## *Manually hyphenating your document*

If you want to decide about each instance of hyphenation, this procedure is for you. If you want to hyphenate only a portion of the document, select that portion first.

1. Choose Tools⇨Hyphenation to open the Hyphenation dialog box when your are ready to begin hyphenating the document.

2. Click the Manual button to have Word begin analyzing the document for hyphenation.

3. To skip a word (that is, don't hyphenate the word), click No.

4. To insert a hyphen at the suggested spot in the word, click Yes.

5. To insert a hyphen at a different spot in the word, click the spot where you want to insert a hyphen.

Because editing affects line breaks, wait until you have finished
editing the document before manually hyphenating.

## More stuff

You can insert nonbreaking hyphens in phrases you want to keep
on one line, such as a hyphenated name or phrase. Nonbreaking
hyphens prevent hyphenated words from breaking at the end of a
line. To insert a nonbreaking hyphen, press Ctrl+Shift+hyphen.

Word also uses optional hyphens. You can use an optional
hyphen when you want to break a word to reduce raggedness.
Then, if editing changes move the word so that the hyphen isn't
necessary, the optional hyphen won't print. To insert an optional
hyphen, press Ctrl+hyphen.

## Indenting

Adds indents to paragraphs to change their position on the page
relative to the margins. Word has three types of indents:

- left indent, where all the lines of the paragraph are indented
  from the left

- right indent, where all the lines of the paragraph are
  indented from the right

- first line indent, where only the first line of the paragraph is
  affected

## For keyboard kut-ups

To indent a paragraph to the next tab stop in the ruler, press

$$\boxed{Ctrl} + \boxed{M}$$

To indent a paragraph to the previous tab stop in the ruler, press

$$\boxed{Ctrl} + \boxed{Shift} + \boxed{M}$$

To apply a hanging indent to a paragraph, press

$$\boxed{Ctrl} + \boxed{T}$$

To remove a hanging indent from a paragraph, press

$$\boxed{Ctrl} + \boxed{Shift} + \boxed{T}$$

## For mouse maniacs

To indent a paragraph to the next tab stop in the ruler, click the Increase Indent button on the Formatting toolbar. To indent a paragraph to the previous tab stop in the ruler, click the Decrease Indent button.

## Setting indents precisely

You can use the Paragraph dialog box to set precise indents. The Preview box displays your choices so that you can adjust them before applying the indents to the selected paragraphs.

1. Choose Format⇨Paragraph to open the Paragraph dialog box; then click the Indents and Spacing tab.

2. To set a left indent, enter a value under Left in the Indentation box. You can enter positive and negative values.

3. To set a right indent, enter a value under Right in the Indentation box. You can enter positive and negative values.

4. To set a first line indent, choose First Line in the Special box and enter a positive or negative value in the By box.

5. To set a hanging indent, choose Hanging in the Special box and enter a positive or negative value in the By box.

6. Click OK to apply the indentation and return to your document.

## Using the horizontal ruler

You can apply any of the indents, positive or negative, by using the horizontal ruler indent markers. Select the paragraph that you want to indent and drag the marker toward the center of the page to increase the indent or toward the edge of the page to reduce the indent. Note that the left indent marker looks like an hourglass on a small pedestal. Drag the top part of the icon to apply a first line indent. Drag the bottom part (the part that looks like the lower half of an hourglass) to apply the indent to every line in the paragraph but the first. Drag the very bottom marker (the part that looks like a small pedestal) to apply the indent to every line in the paragraph, including the first.

## More stuff

Positive indents increase the space from the margins. Negative indents position the text closer to the edges of the page. You can apply negative indents only by using the Paragraph dialog box or the horizontal ruler indent markers.

## Indexing

Creates an index for longer Word documents. In Word, indexes, tables of contents, tables of figures, and tables of authorities are similar. They all require three basic steps: you select (mark) the entries, choose a format, and compile the index or table. They all use fields that Word searches for to compile the index or table.

## For keyboard kut-ups

To open the Mark Index Entry dialog box, press

## Creating (marking) index entries

Marking index entries is the first step in creating your index.

1. Select the text you want to mark as an index entry.

2. Press Alt+Shift+X to open the Mark Index Entry dialog box. The selected text appears in the Main Entry box.

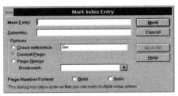

3. Accept this text or change it. You can format this text by selecting it in the Main Entry box and using the appropriate shortcut keystrokes.

4. To create a subentry, type the text in the Subentry box. You can format this text by selecting it in the Subentry box and using the appropriate shortcut keystrokes.

5. To create a cross-reference for the index entry in the Main Entry box, enable the Cross-reference option and type the cross-reference.

6. To list the current page number for the index entry, enable the Current Page option. Word chooses this option by default.

7. To specify a range of pages for the index entry, enable the Page Range Bookmark option. However, you must have

previously created a bookmark that covers the range you want. If you have, then type that bookmark name in this box.

8. Choose a format for the page number that will appear in the index (Bold or Italic).

9. To mark the index entry, click the Mark button. The dialog box stays open so that you can go back to the document and continue to mark indexes.

10. If you select an entry that occurs a number of times in the document and you want Word to mark an index entry for each occurrence, click the Mark All button.

11. When you have finished marking all the index entries, click the Close button.

## Formatting and compiling an index

You cannot compile an index unless you first create index entries.

1. Place the insertion point where you want the index in your document.

2. Choose Insert⇨Index and Tables to open the Index and Tables dialog box.

3. Click the Index tab.

4. Choose either Indented or Run-in under Type. Indented places a subentry on a line below the main entry; Run-in places a subentry on the same line.

5. Choose the format you want in the Formats box. The Preview box shows an example of your choice.

6. To right-align page numbers, enable the Right Align Page Numbers option. The Preview box reflects this choice.

7. Choose from 1 to 4 Columns for your index. The default is whatever column formatting your document uses.

8. If you enabled the Right Align Page Numbers option, choose a tab leader from the Tab Leader box. Any tab leader you choose is shown in the Preview box.

9. Click OK to compile the index.

## Automatically marking index entries

Generally, when you mark an index entry, the index lists a single page reference for that entry. Sometimes, though, you have an entry that appears frequently throughout your document, and you want the index to list all the page references. If you have a lot of entries that fall into this category, you can automate the index marking process.

The way you do this is to create a file that contains a table of those entries and how you want each of them to appear in the index. This is called a *concordance file.* The concordance file consists of a two-column table, with the first column listing each entry and the second column listing how you want that entry to appear in the index. Then, when you want to mark all those entries for your index, you open the concordance file, and Word marks the entries for you based on what the file contains. This approach relieves you of having to search out each instance of the entry in the document that you index.

## Creating a concordance file

1. Click the New button on the Standard toolbar to create a new file.

2. Choose Table⇨Insert Table to open the Insert Table dialog box.

3. Click OK to accept the default of 2 columns and 2 rows. Word inserts the table in the new document. The insertion point is in the first cell.

4. Type the entry you want Word to mark in the document that is to be indexed. Remember that what you type must exactly match the text in the document to be indexed, including capitalization.

5. Press Tab to move to the next cell and type the entry as you want it to appear in the index. If you want it to appear as you typed it in the first column, press F4.

6. Press Tab to move to the next row.

7. Repeat steps 4 – 6 for each entry.

8. When you have listed all the entries, save the file as you would any other file.

## Using the concordance file

1. Open the document to be indexed.

2. Choose <u>I</u>nsert⇨Inde<u>x</u> and Tables to open the Index and Tables dialog box.

3. Click the Inde<u>x</u> tab.

4. Click the A<u>u</u>toMark button to open the Open Index AutoMark File dialog box. This dialog box looks and functions just the same as the File Open dialog box.

5. Change the drive and directory, if necessary, and choose the concordance file.

6. Click OK. Word automatically marks every instance of each item you included in the concordance file.

## More stuff

 Index entries and indexes themselves are fields. Index entries are formatted as hidden, so you cannot see them unless you display hidden text (see **Hidden Text**). However, in order to be sure of the accuracy of your index, you should be careful not to display or print hidden text when you compile the index. Displaying or printing hidden text causes Word to include the hidden text as part of the document and thus affects the pagination.

 You can create index entries by inserting index fields directly, if you wish, but you need to know something about fields and switches. For more on indexing and fields, see *Word For Windows 6 For Dummies.*

## Inserting a File into the Current File

Inserts the contents of another file into the current file.

## Inserting a file

1. Position the insertion point where you want to insert the contents of the other file.

2. Choose <u>I</u>nsert⇨Fi<u>l</u>e to open the File dialog box. This dialog box looks and functions the same as the File Open dialog box.

3. Change the drive and directory if necessary.

4. If you aren't sure of the location of the file, click the Find File button to open the File Find dialog box. (See **File Find.**)

5. Select the file you want to insert.

6. If the file you want to insert is from another application and you want to confirm the file conversion to Word's format, enable the Confirm Conversions option.

7. If you want to establish a link to the original file, enable the Link to File option. *Linking* means that changes made to the original file are also made to the copy in the Word document.

8. You can insert part of the file (the Range), but only if you previously created a bookmark in that file. The bookmark must include the part you want to insert. If this is the case, type the bookmark name in the Range box and only that part of the file will be inserted.

9. Click OK to insert to file (or part of the file).

## More stuff

You can insert only document and text files using this procedure; you cannot insert graphics.

When you insert a file into the current file, the incoming file's styles are merged with the styles in the current file. This combination can make the list of styles in the current document grow substantially, especially if you use this procedure frequently.

## Inserting Objects

Embeds or links graphics and other objects into the current document. Word's Insert Object command opens the door to a whole new dimension of elements you can include in your documents. Although the terminology is relatively new and may seem confusing, this stuff really isn't hard to use.

*Object* is simply the term used for the information that is exchanged between and among applications. Objects can include text, documents, images, charts, tables, and, more recently, voice annotations and video clips. If you have never used some of these things, it is no big deal. But if you ever want to incorporate them into a Word document, you have the capability.

Inserting an object can mean using another application to create the object and then embedding it in your document. Or, it can mean retrieving an already existing object from a graphic or other file and embedding or linking it.

## Creating and inserting a new object

1. Choose Insert⇨Object to open the Object dialog box.

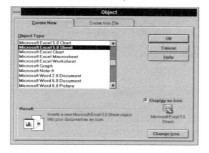

2. Click the Create New tab. Applications that Word can exchange information with appear in the Object Type box.

3. Choose the application you want to use to create the new object.

4. If you want to display the object you create as an icon in your document rather than display the object itself, enable the Display as Icon option. If you enable this option, the Change Icon button appears; you can click this button to choose a different icon.

5. Click OK. Word closes the dialog box and opens the application you chose.

6. Create the object in the application. When you finish, click OK or choose Update from the File menu. The object you created is inserted in Word as an embedded object.

7. To edit the object, just double-click it. The original application opens and you can edit the object.

## Inserting an existing file as an object

You cannot use this method to insert part of a file; rather, you must insert the entire file.

1. Choose Insert⇨Object to open the Object dialog box.

2. Click the Create from File tab. This dialog box looks and functions in the same manner as the File Open dialog box.

3. Change the drive and directory if necessary.

4. If you aren't sure of the location of the file, click the Find File button to open the File Find dialog box. (See **File Find.**)

5. Select the file you want to insert.

6. If you want to link the file rather than embed it, enable the Link To File option.

7. If you want to display the object you create as an icon in your document rather than display the object itself, enable the Display as Icon option. If you enable this option, the Change Icon button appears; you can click this button to choose a different icon.

8. Click OK to insert the contents of the file as an object.

9. Editing the object depends on whether you inserted it as an embedded object or a linked object. If you inserted it as embedded, just double-click on the object to open the original application and edit. If you linked it, you can edit it by opening the original file independently and making the changes to that file. Those changes are reflected in the object in the current file.

## More stuff

Although linking and embedding are complex topics, using them is easy. It's more important to be able to use them than to understand all the underlying concepts, so don't get hung up on the terminology. And, as with so many features in Word, the best way to become familiar with these features is to experiment.

 When you link, the object in your document is linked to an object in another document, and you can update them both at the same time by editing the original. When you embed, the object in your document stands alone, but it contains all the information necessary to modify it. All you have to do is double-click it to open the application that created the object and then use that application's tools to modify it.

 For more on linking and embedding, see **Linking** and **OLE** in this guide.

 For a more comprehensive treatment of this topic, see *Word For Windows 6 For Dummies.*

## Inserting Pictures

Inserts a graphic file from another application. This command is only one of several ways to import a graphic into your document.

# Inserting a picture

1. Position the insertion point where you want to insert the picture.

2. Choose Insert⇨Picture to open the Insert Picture dialog box. This dialog box looks and functions similarly to the File Open dialog box.

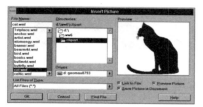

3. Change the drive and directory if necessary. If you aren't sure where the picture is stored, click the Find File button to open the Find File dialog box. (See **File Find.**)

4. Select a file in the File Name box.

5. To list specific graphic file types, change the List Files of Type. The default is All Graphics files.

6. To create a link to the original file, enable the Link to File option. *Linking* means that changes made to the original file are also made to the copy in the Word document.

7. If you enable the Link to File option, the Save Picture in Document option becomes available. Clearing this option means that Word stores a graphic representation of the picture in your document rather than the picture itself. This practice can considerably reduce the size of your document file.

8. Click OK to insert the picture and close the dialog box.

# More stuff

Choosing the Link to File option and clearing the Save Picture in File option offers the major benefit of reducing the size of your document. Instead of storing the actual graphic, Word stores a field that links to the original graphic and a copy of the graphic. The net result is that the same graphic prints in your document, but without increasing the size of your document. Unless you have a compelling reason to store the actual graphic in your document, you should always choose the Link to File option and clear the Save Picture in File option.

For more on linking and embedding, see **Linking** and **OLE** in this guide.

For a more comprehensive treatment of this topic, see *Word For Windows 6 For Dummies.*

## *Italics*

Adds italics to selected text.

Italics are character attributes, which means you first must select the characters before you can italicize them, unlike paragraph attributes, where you need only be in the paragraph. See **Font Formatting** for more on this topic.

### *For keyboard kut-ups*

Select the text and press

 **+**

### *For mouse maniacs*

Select the text and click the Italic button on the Formatting toolbar.

## *Applying italics to text as you type*

1. Press Ctrl+I or click the Italics button on the Formatting toolbar. All the characters you type will be italicized.

2. To turn italics off, repeat step 1.

## *Keeping Lines and Paragraphs Together*

Prevents page breaks from occurring between selected lines and paragraphs. If you want all the lines of a paragraph to appear on the same page, you can format them so that a page break won't separate them. If a page break normally would have occurred in the paragraph, Word moves the entire paragraph to the next page. You can also format consecutive paragraphs so that a page break won't occur within them. This method is most commonly applied to a heading and the paragraph that follows the heading.

## Keeping lines together

1. Place the insertion point in the paragraph you want to keep on a page.

2. Choose Format⇨Paragraph to open the Paragraph dialog box; then click the Text Flow tab.

3. Enable Keep Lines Together under Pagination.

4. Click OK.

## Keeping paragraphs together

1. If you want to keep two paragraphs together, place the insertion point in the first paragraph. If you want to keep more than two paragraphs together, select all but the last paragraph.

2. Choose Format⇨Paragraph to open the Paragraph dialog box; then click the Text Flow tab.

3. Enable the Keep With Next option.

4. Click OK.

## More stuff

A common error is to enable either of these two options as the document is created and forget to disable the option. Not disabling these options causes Word to insert a page break between every paragraph. This, in turn, can have quite a negative impact on things like a table of contents and an index. The best way to use this feature is to create the document, do all or most of the necessary editing, and then apply the keep together options as needed for specific paragraphs.

Keeping lines and paragraphs together is part of paragraph formatting. For more on this topic, see **Paragraph Formatting.**

## Keyboard Shortcuts (Assigning)

Lets you assign keyboard shortcuts to any command, macro, font, AutoText entry, style, or special character. Word also lets you change any current key assignment, even the defaults.

## Assigning keystrokes to commands

1. Choose Tools⇨Customize to open the Customize dialog box; then click the Keyboard tab.

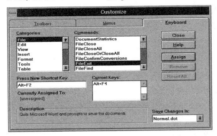

2. Choose the category in the Categories box that contains the command you want to assign the keystroke to. Scroll to the bottom to see items other than menu commands.

3. Choose the command in the Commands box. If the command currently has a keystroke assigned, that keystroke appears in the Current Keys box. You can choose a different keystroke.

4. Click in the Press New Shortcut Key box and type the proposed keystroke. Word inserts the keystroke you type in the box. Word also displays the current use of that keystroke or informs you that it is unassigned. Whether or not the keystroke you typed is currently assigned to another function, you can assign it to the command you chose in the Commands box.

5. Click the Assign button to assign the keystroke you typed to the command you chose.

6. Choose the template you want to save the changes to in the Save Changes In box.

7. When you have assigned all the keystrokes you want, click Close.

## More stuff

Assigning keystroke shortcuts to commands is quick and easy in Word and makes life a whole lot easier. One minor drawback is that using someone else's computer will be more difficult. Also, if you reassign the default keystrokes for your own use, other people using your computer will generate errors when they use the default keystrokes. For these reasons, assigning shortcut keystrokes to a template other than the Normal template is a good practice.

## Labels

Lets you print a single label or a sheet of address labels with a single address, such as a return address.

If you want to create mailing labels to use in a merge, see **Mail Merges.**

## Printing mailing labels

This procedure lets you print a single address label or a sheet of labels that contains a single address.

1. Choose Tools⊅Envelopes and Labels to open the Envelopes and Labels dialog box; then click the Labels tab.

2. Accept the address that Word has inserted, if any, or type an address in the Address box.

3. If you want Word to use the address that is stored in User Info (see **User Information**), enable the Use Return Address option. If you enable this option and type another address in the Address box, Word asks you if you want to use the address you typed as the new User Info default.

4. If you have a printer that prints bar codes, you can enable the Delivery Point Bar Code option. This prints the POSTNET bar code that allows postal machines to read the zip code.

5. Choose Eull Page or Single label in the Print box. If you choose Single Label, specify what Row and Column you want to print the label on. The Label box shows the current label choice.

6. If you want to change the type of label, click the Options button to open the Label Options dialog box. See the table that follows for an explanation of this dialog box.

7. To print the label or labels, click the Print button.

8. To save the label or labels as a table, click the New Document button and then save the label document as you would any other Word document.

## Languages

Changes the keyboard layout and proofs your Word document in another language. This procedure requires that you purchase a language module for each foreign language that you want to use. Call Microsoft Customer Service for more information on this topic; choose Help⇨Technical Support.

## Checking Text in Other Languages

Word allows you to run spell checks for text written in languages other than English. You need to purchase and install a separate language dictionary for each language you want to check to use this option. Then you can mark selected text to be checked in the other languages.

## Checking spelling with a foreign language dictionary

1. Select the text you want to mark in the other language.

2. Choose Tools⇨Language to open the Language dialog box.

3. Choose the language in the Mark Selected Text As box and click OK. You can now check this text using the other language's dictionary.

For more on dictionaries, see **Spelling Checker.**

## More stuff

You can include languages in your styles so that selected paragraphs are formatted as another language.

---

## Line Breaks

Inserts a line break in your text. So what's a line break? A *line break* is what you do when you want to continue typing on the next line but you don't want to press Enter to create a paragraph. Some systems refer to a line break as a *soft return*.

## Inserting a line break

To insert a line break, just press Shift+Enter. Word inserts a line break wherever the insertion point happens to be. The line break symbol looks like the small arrow next to the word Enter on the Enter key (although you can't see it unless you click on the Show/Hide button on the Standard toolbar).

## More stuff

A line break, or soft return, does not create a new paragraph. When you apply any paragraph formatting to a paragraph that contains a line break, the entire paragraph, including the text that follows the line break, receives the formatting.

---

## Line Numbering

Adds consecutive numbers to each line of text in a section or document. If you decide to add line numbering to a section or document, Word does not apply the line numbers to tables, footnotes, endnotes, frames, headers, and footers.

## Adding line numbers to text

1. Place the insertion point in the section where you want to apply line numbers. If the document consists of only one section, the entire document gets the line numbers.

2. Choose File⇨Page Setup to open the Page Setup dialog box; then click on the Layout tab.

3. Click on the Line Numbers button to open the Line Numbers dialog box.

4. Enable the Add Line Numbering option to make all the other options available.

5. If you want the line numbering to start with a number other than 1, enter that number in the Start At box.

6. Specify the distance between the number and the text by entering a value in the From Text box.

7. To add line numbers in increments other than 1 (such as 1, 3, 5, 7,...), enter the increment in the Count By box.

8. Choose the numbering option you want in the Numbering box.

9. Click OK to return to the Page Setup dialog box.

10. In the Page Setup dialog box, specify what part of the document gets the line numbers by making a choice in the Apply To box to the right of the Line Numbers button. You can select the entire document, the current section (if the document has more than one section), or from the current point forward in the document.

## More stuff

Line numbering is part of section formatting. For more on this topic, see **Sections.**

Line numbers are printed in the left margin (or between columns, if the section or document is formatted with columns). If the margins are too small, the line numbers do not print.

Line numbers are not visible in normal view. To be able to see the line numbers, switch to page layout view or print preview.

## Line Spacing

Adjust the amount of space between the lines in a paragraph. Line spacing is one of the elements of paragraph formatting, but because it is so important, it is treated here as a separate topic.

Most people think of line spacing as single- or double-spaced lines, and that suffices in most cases. However, Word offers more options than just those basic ones.

# For keyboard kut-ups

To apply single-spacing to a paragraph, press

To apply double-spacing to a paragraph, press

To apply 1.5 line spacing to a paragraph, press

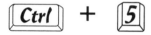

(Note that you must type these numbers from the number keys above the letter keys on your keyboard, *not* from the numeric keypad on the right. If you use the numeric keypad, you get different results.)

# Adjusting line spacing

1. Position the insertion point in the paragraph where you want to adjust the line spacing.

2. Choose Format⇨Paragraph to open the Paragraph dialog box; then click the Indents and Spacing tab.

3. Choose the line spacing option you want in the Line Spacing box.

4. To specify an exact amount of line spacing, enter a value in the At box. You can enter precise values here, such as 2.35.

5. Click OK to apply the line spacing to the selected paragraph and close the dialog box.

## *More stuff*

Line spacing is one element of paragraph formatting. For more on the other elements, see **Paragraph Formatting.**

## *Linking*

Lets you insert and link objects created in other applications. *Linking* means that you can edit the object in its original application and that the edits are reflected in your Word document as well. You can also link between Word documents so that changes made to the original are transmitted automatically to the copied and linked object.

Linked objects imply the existence of the object in at least two places: the file where it was created and your Word document. The object can be copied and linked to any Windows application that supports linking (and almost all do). The great advantage to linking is that you can edit the object once, in the source application, and the edits occur automatically in all the linked objects.

## *Creating a link*

To create a link in another application, you must have both Word and the source application running.

1. Switch to the source application (that is, the application in which you want to create the object). For example, if you want to link a table from Excel, switch to Excel.

2. In the source application, create and select the object. If it already exists, select it.

3. In the source application, choose Edit⇨Copy. This places the selected object on the Clipboard.

4. Switch to your Word document and position the insertion point where you want to insert the linked object.

5. Edit⇨Paste Special to open the Paste Special dialog box. The options in the dialog box vary, depending on the application you use to create the object and on what type of object you create (a graphic, a table, a paragraph, and so on).

6. Choose the Paste Link option.

7. In the As box, choose the type of link you want.

8. Click OK to insert the object and establish the link.

## Creating a link from within Word

You can also create a link without leaving Word by using Insert⇨Object. When you use this method, Word opens the other application for you, and when you close the other application, you automatically return to Word. This procedure is explained under **Inserting Objects**.

## Editing linked objects

It is important to remember to edit linked information in the original application so that the information is consistent in both the source file and all the destination files.

1. In your Word document, choose the linked information you want to edit.

2. From the Edit menu choose the name of the link, such as Excel link or Picture link. (This choice is at the bottom of the Edit menu unless it's been modified.) This opens a drop-down menu.

3. Choose Edit from the drop-down menu. Word opens the source application.

4. Make the changes you want to make in the other application and save the file.

## More stuff

Linked objects are stored in Word as fields. You can see a field code by choosing Tools⇨Options and then clicking the View tab and enabling Field Codes, or by pressing Alt+F9. (This is also true of embedding.)

Although there are several methods for updating a link, by far the easiest is to choose the link and press F9. To update all the links in a document quickly, select the entire document and press F9. (Don't use this approach, though, if you have other fields in the document that you don't want to update. Pressing F9 updates all fields, not just links.)

You can change the linked object itself in Word and transmit the change back to the source file. Select the changes linked information and press Ctrl+Shift+F7.

For more on linking and embedding, see **Inserting Objects** and **OLE**.

For more on linking and embedding, see *Word For Windows 6 For Dummies*.

## *Macros*

Lets you record a series of keystrokes to automate your tasks.
You can then assign the macro to a keystroke, toolbar, or menu.
Typical uses for macros include combining a series of commands,
speeding up routine editing and formatting, and automating
complex tasks.

The macro language in Word is actually quite sophisticated.
Professional developers use Word's macro language (known as
WordBasic) to create specialized functions for clients, and entire
books have been devoted to just the macro language in Word.
The Help feature in Word covers lists and explains all the
commands in WordBasic, but it doesn't tell you how to put them
together to create a program.

Fortunately, Word comes with a macro recorder. You can use the
macro recorder to record a series of actions, including typing
text, formatting, and using menu commands, to make your work
easier. The macro recorder actually translates your actions into
Word's macro language. You can give your recorded macro a
name and assign it to a menu, put it on a toolbar, or simply give it
a keystroke combination. If the macro is on a toolbar, it is easy to
find and run.

Try a simple macro first. For example, record a macro when you
select a sentence using keystrokes and then bold the sentence.
Assign a keystroke to the macro and then run it. Macros can be
easy to record and even kind of fun, especially when they take the
drudgery out of repetitive tasks for you.

## *For mouse maniacs*

To open the Record Macro dialog box, double-click on the REC
box on the status bar.

## *Recording a macro*

1. Choose Tools⇨Macro to open the Macro dialog box.
2. Click the Record button to open the Record Macro dialog box.

3. Type a name for the macro in the Record Macro Name box. You can't use spaces, commas, or periods. You can accept Word's suggestion.

4. If the current document is using a template other than Normal, choose either the current template or the Normal template.

5. If you want to include a description of the macro, type the description in the Description box. Any description you type appears in the status bar if you assign the macro to a menu or toolbar button.

6. Choose one of the buttons (Toolbars, Menus, or Keyboard) for assigning the macro. Any button you choose opens the Custom dialog box, where you can click the tabs to assign the macro to all three items (a toolbar, menu, and keystroke).

7. Click the Close button to close the dialog box and begin recording your macro. Note that the two-button Macro toolbar appears. The left button stops the recording when you have finished, and the right button pauses the recording if you need to interrupt it.

8. Perform the actions that you want to record.

9. When you finish recording, either click the Stop button on the Macro toolbar or double-click the REC indicator in the status bar.

## *Running a macro*

The easiest way to run a macro is to use a keystroke, click a button on a toolbar, or choose it from a menu. When you begin recording a macro, Word lets you make running it easy. The Record Macro dialog box has buttons to open the Customize dialog box. However, you can also run a macro even if you didn't assign a keystroke to it or put it on a menu or a toolbar.

1. Choose Tools⇨Macro to open the Macro dialog box. All the macros contained in the current template are listed in the box on the left.

2. Choose the macro you want to run.

3. Click the Run button to run the macro.

## *More stuff*

You can also edit and delete customized macros in the Macro dialog box. However, unless you are familiar with Word's macro language, you should not edit or delete any macro you haven't created yourself.

The macro recorder cannot record mouse actions when you work in text, so you must use keystrokes when recording a macro. However, you can use the mouse to choose menu commands and make selections in dialog boxes.

For more on customizing, see **Keyboard Shortcuts, Menus**, and **Toolbars.**

For more on using macros in Word, see *Word For Windows 6 For Dummies.*

## Mail Merges

Lets you send a letter or other document to a number of different addresses. A mail merge in Word involves two documents: the *main document* and the *data document*. The main document is the letter or other document you want to send. The data document is a list of the names and addresses to which you want to send the main document. You can keep the data document in a Word table, or you can get the information from a different source, such as Excel or a database application.

For more on getting information from a database application, see **Databases.**

A quick review is probably in order here. A database (or, as Word calls it, a data document) consists of *records*. Each merge letter that you print contains information from a single record. Records are composed of elements called *fields*. All the records in a database have the same structure; that is, they all consist of the same fields. Each record in your data document, for example, might have a first name field, a last name field, a company field, an address field, and so on. The first record in the database is called the *header record*. The header record is simply a record that contains the field names of the records.

The process requires three basic steps: first, you create the main document (or use an existing one); next, you set up the data source, which can be a table in Word or an outside source; finally, you merge the two. (Many more steps may be involved, depending on whether or not you already have a data document or need to create one and whether you already have a main document with merge codes or the codes need to be inserted.)

When you perform a merge, Word displays one Merge toolbar for the main document and a different Merge toolbar for the data document (since they have different roles in a merge and require different functions). The toolbars have buttons designed to make merging simple.

## *Merging letters*

1. If you already have a letter you want to use as the main document, open it. If not, create a new file.

2. Choose Tools⇔Mail Merge to open the Mail Merge Helper dialog box. Note the advice at the top of the dialog box that instructs you to choose the Create button.

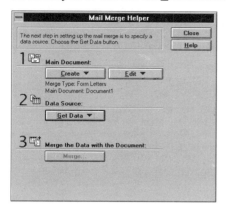

3. When you click the Create button, a pull-down menu appears. Choose Form Letters.

4. In the dialog box that now appears, click the Active Window button. The active window becomes a merge document and returns you to the Mail Merge Helper dialog box, which now advises you to create or open the data source.

5. Click the Get Data button and then choose Open Data Source from the drop-down menu. This opens the Open Data Source dialog box, which looks and functions similarly to the File Open dialog box. (If you need to create a data source, see the next set of instructions.)

6. Change the drive and directory, if necessary, to choose your data file. (This step attaches the data document to your main document.)

7. If your main document doesn't already have the merge fields inserted, click the Edit Main Document button as directed by a Word message. Word opens the main document and displays the Merge Main Document toolbar.

8. Position the insertion point where you want to begin inserting the codes. For example, to insert codes to create an address block, position the insertion point where you want the address block in the merged letters to appear.

9. Click the Insert Merge Field button on the Merge toolbar. A drop-down menu consisting of a list of the data fields in your data document appears.

10. Choose the data field codes you want. In an address block, for example, you might choose a FirstName code, press the spacebar, and then choose a LastName code. Then press Enter, choose a JobTitle code, press Enter again, and then choose a Company code. In this way you can build an address block of codes. Word inserts the data from the data file when you actually begin the merge and creates a new letter for each record you merge.

11. Click the Check For Errors button to have Word check for errors such as incorrect field names. Now you are ready to begin your merge.

12. When you merge, you can merge to a new document or to the printer. It is always best to merge at least some records to a new document, which appears on your screen. This test is a quick and easy way to catch errors before you begin printing the merged letters. To merge to a new document, click the Merge To New Document button. To merge to the printer, click the Merge To Printer button.

## Creating a data document during a merge

You can, of course, create a data document any time by creating a table and entering records. Word also lets you create a data document on the fly, so to speak.

1. Follow steps 1 – 4 for merging letters.

2. Click on the Create Data Source button in item 2 in the Mail Merge Helper dialog box and then choose Create Data Source. This opens the Create Data Source dialog box.

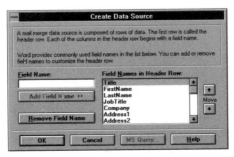

3. Word provides a list of common field names in the Field Names In Header Row box. Scroll to see the entire list.

4. To delete a field name, choose it and click the Remove Field Name button. Word removes the field name from the Field Names In Header Row box and inserts it in the Field Name box. You can type a new field name, which must begin with a letter and cannot contain any spaces. You can use letters, numbers, and underscores in a field name, which can be up to 40 characters.

5. Click the Add Field Name button to add the new field name you typed.

6. To change the order of the field names, choose a field name in the Field Names In Header Row box and click the up or down arrow repeatedly to move it to a new position.

7. When you finish creating the field names you want, click OK. This opens the Save Data Source dialog box, which functions similarly to the File Save As dialog box.

8. Choose a drive and directory and give the data file a name and then click OK. Word displays a message asking whether you want to edit the Data source or the Main document.

9. Click the Edit Data Source button to begin building the data document.

## Merging mailing labels

If you already have a mailing label main document, you won't need to create one. However, this procedure assumes you need to create a new one. If you already have one, open it and make it the active document. In step 3, below, choose Active Document.

1. Choose Tools⇨Mail Merge to open the Mail Merge Helper dialog box.

2. Click the Create button to display a pull-down menu. Choose Mailing Labels. Word prompts you to either use the active document or create a new one.

3. Choose New Main Document Window. Word opens a new document for you.

4. Click the Get Data button and then choose Open Data Source from the drop-down menu. This opens the Open Data Source dialog box, which looks and functions similarly to the File Open dialog box. (If you need to create a data source, see the previous set of instructions.)

5. Change the drive and directory, if necessary, to choose your data file. Choose the file and click OK. Word displays a message that your main document needs to be set up.

6. Click the Set Up Main Document button, which opens the Label Options dialog box.

7. Specify the labels you want to use. (For an explanation of this dialog box, see **Labels.**)

8. Click OK, and Word opens the Create Labels dialog box. Click in the Sample Label box to position the insertion point there.

9. Click the Insert Merge Field button to begin inserting the merge fields. Type spaces and any punctuation you want between the merge fields and press Enter at the end of each line.

10. When you have finished entering the fields, click OK to close the dialog box. You can now begin merging your labels.

11. When you merge, you can merge to a new document or to the printer. It is always best to merge at least some records to a new document, which appears on your screen. This test is a quick and easy way to catch errors before you begin printing the merged letters. To merge to a new document, click the Merge To New Document button. To merge to the printer, click the Merge To Printer button.

## Merging envelopes

Merging envelopes is almost exactly the same as merging labels. The only real difference is that in step 6, Word displays the Envelope Options dialog box instead of the Label Options dialog box. You can use this dialog box to choose different envelope sizes, the fonts you want to use for the return and mailing addresses, and the positioning of the return and mailing addresses.

## Removing an attached data source

When you attach a data file to a main document, the two stay attached until you remove the attachment.

1. In the Mail Merge Helper dialog box, open the main document that is attached to the data file. Because it is still attached to the data file, Word displays the Merge toolbar.

2. Click the Create button under Main Document.

3. Choose Restore to Normal Document.

4. Click Yes to Word's confirmation message.

5. Close the Mail Merge Helper dialog box.

## More stuff

Mail merges can now be used to merge information by using electronic mail systems and fax machines. For more on using the Mail Merge feature in Word, see *Word For Windows 6 For Dummies.*

## Margins

Sets margins on any page of your document. The default margins in Word are 1.0 inch for the top and bottom margins, and 1.25 inches for the left and right margins. You can change margin settings for the entire document, a section of the document, or a selection of paragraphs.

## Changing margins using Page Setup

1. If you want to change the margins for selected text, select the text. If you want to change the margins for a particular section, be sure the insertion point is in that section.

2. Choose File⇨Page Setup to open the Page Setup dialog box and click the Margins tab.

3. Enter the margin sizes you want.

4. Select the part of the document that you want to apply the margin change to and click OK.

## Changing margins using the rulers

You can reset the margins by dragging the margin boundaries on the horizontal and vertical rulers. To use the rulers to change margins, you must be in either page layout view or print preview. (You cannot even see the vertical ruler in normal view.)

1. Switch to either page layout view or print preview.

2. Position the insertion point in the section where you want to change the margins. If the document has only one section, the margins are changed for the entire document.

3. Drag the margin boundaries on the horizontal ruler to change the left and right margins; drag the margin boundaries on the vertical ruler to change the top and bottom margins. If you carefully position the pointer on the line that separates the white area of the ruler from the gray area, it becomes a double-headed arrow. You can then drag the boundary to change the margins.

You can display the measurements of the text area and the margins as you drag by pressing Alt at the same time.

## More stuff

The Page Setup dialog box offers more options in setting margins than using the rulers. For example, you can apply margin changes to selected text using the dialog box, and Word inserts the necessary section breaks for you. You can also apply the margin changes from the current point forward in the document. And you can specify that the margin changes apply to the entire document regardless of how many sections are in the document.

If you want to change the margins for selected text with the rulers, first insert a section break before and after the text and then position the insertion point in the newly created section. You can now use the rulers to change margins, specifically in that section.

## Master Documents

Lets you organize a long document by dividing it into smaller subdocuments. Any Word document can be a master document or a subdocument. When you use a master document, you can work with the entire long document or with any of the individual subdocuments. Word has a master document view that you can use when you work with master documents, or you can use any other view as you wish. The master document view is very similar to the outline view. You can create a master document either from scratch or from an existing long document.

## Creating a new master document

1. Create a new document.

2. Choose View⇨Master Document to switch to master document view. The Outline and Master Document toolbars are now available.

3. Type your outline for the master document. In other words, type the headings for the entire long document.

4. Format the headings with Word's built-in heading styles. This step is important, because Word uses these styles when it builds subdocuments.

5. Select the headings you want to divide into subdocuments. Word uses whatever heading level you first select to determine which heading levels become subdocuments. For example, if you first select heading level 2, Word creates a new subdocument each time it encounters another heading level 2.

6. Click the Create Subdocument button on the Master Document toolbar. Each subdocument is enclosed in a box and separated by a section break. Word also displays a subdocument icon in the upper-left hand corner of each subdocument box.

7. File⇨Save As to save the new master document and all the subdocuments.

8. Type a file name, choose a location for the new master document, and click OK. Word assigns a file name to each of the subdocuments based on the first characters of the heading that begins the subdocument.

## Converting an existing document to a master document

The only difference between this procedure and creating a new master document from scratch is that, instead of typing the heading, you use the existing headings in your document. When you open the existing document, use the buttons on the Outlining toolbar to promote, demote, and arrange the headings and then select the headings you want to divide into subdocuments. Word uses whatever heading level you first select to determine which heading levels become subdocuments. For example, if you first select heading level 2, Word creates a new subdocument each time it encounters another heading level 2.

## Inserting an existing Word document into a master document

1. Open the master document and switch to master document view.

2. Position the insertion point where you want to add the existing document.

3. Click the Insert Subdocument button on the Master Document toolbar.

4. Enter the file name of the document you want to insert in the File Name box.

5. Click OK to have Word add the document. The new subdocument keeps its original name.

## More stuff

The concept of master documents can be a real help if you must work with long documents. Long documents in Word aren't rigidly defined, but if your document is more than 25 or 30 pages, you might want to consider using a master document.

For more on working with master documents, see *Word For Windows 6 For Dummies*.

# Menus

Add commands, macros, fonts, AutoText, and styles to menus. You can use this feature to customize your menus. If you use different templates, you can customize the menus separately for each template. You can also add your own menus to the menu bar.

## Assigning commands or other items to a menu

1. Choose Tools⇨Customize to open the Customize dialog box and then click the Menus tab.

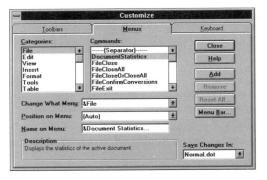

2. Choose the Category that contains the command or other item you want to add to a menu. Scroll to the bottom to choose macros, fonts, AutoText, and styles in the Categories box.

3. In the box to the right of the Categories box (which changes its label depending on the category you choose), choose the command or other item you want to add.

4. Choose the menu you want to assign the item to in the Change What Menu box.

5. Choose the position on the menu where you want to add the item in the Position on Menu box. You can choose Auto (lets Word position similar items together), At Top, At Bottom, or any existing item on the menu. If you select an existing item, the item you add is inserted above the existing one.

6. Type the name you want to appear on the menu in the Name on Menu box or accept the default that Word suggests.

7. Click the Add (or Add Below) button to add the item to the chosen menu. The dialog box stays open so you can add more items.

## Removing items from a menu

Removing any item from a menu is really simple in Word, especially in comparison to adding items (which in itself isn't so bad). To remove an item from a menu, press Alt+Ctrl+hyphen. The mouse pointer becomes a bold minus sign. Open any menu and click on an item. Boom! Word makes that item disappear. (You can, of course, use the Customize menu to remove items from menus, but why bother?)

## Adding, deleting, and renaming menus

You can add entire new menus and delete existing menus in Word. If you delete a menu, you also delete all the submenus under it, so be careful. You can add as many menus as you like, depending on your computer's memory configuration and the space on your screen. You can also rename any existing menu.

1. Choose Tools⇔Customize to open the Customize dialog box and then click the Menus tab.

2. Click the Menu Bar button to open the Menu Bar dialog box.

3. To add or rename a menu, type the name in the <u>N</u>ame on Menu Bar box. As soon as you type the name, the <u>A</u>dd button becomes available.

4. To add the new menu name to the menu bar, click the <u>A</u>dd button.

5. To rename a menu, select it in the <u>P</u>osition on Menu Bar box and then click the R<u>e</u>name button. Word renames the selected menu with whatever you typed in the <u>N</u>ame on Menu Bar box.

6. To delete an existing menu, select it in the <u>P</u>osition on Menu Bar box. Click the <u>R</u>emove button to delete the menu item with all its submenus.

## More stuff

You may have already noticed that each menu command in Word has one underlined character. This is the keystroke character. If you press Alt and type the underlined character in the menu of your choice on the menu bar, the list of submenus opens. Note that each submenu item also has an underlined character. Typing this character (without pressing any other keys) causes Word to execute that command.

When you add menu items and menus, you might want to create underlined characters so that you can use keystroke shortcuts. You can create these shortcuts by typing an ampersand (&) in front of the character you want to underline. This technique applies to both menu names and submenus. The only thing you must be careful of is to not have two of the same underlined characters in the same menu.

## *Nonprinting Characters*

Refers to characters you may want to see on your screen but that do not print as part of your document. Included in this category are paragraph marks, tabs, spaces between words, and any other element that isn't typewritten text. To view nonprinting characters, click the Show/Hide button on the Standard toolbar. Clicking the Show/Hide button also toggles the display of any hidden text in your document.

See **Hidden Text.**

# OLE (Object Linking and Embedding)

Lets you import graphic and other objects into your Word document. You can link and embed these objects. OLE is a set of methods that lets you exchange information between and among Windows applications in a variety of ways.

*Linking* means creating the object in another application, copying it to the Clipboard, and then paste linking it in your Word document. Linking uses Dynamic Data Exchange, or DDE, so that when you make changes to the original copy, those changes are also made to the linked copy in the Word document.

*Embedding* means creating an object in another application and then storing the object and all the information needed to edit that object in your Word document. The object doesn't exist outside your Word document (and anywhere else you embed it). To edit an embedded object, you simply double-click on the object. That action opens the application that created the object so that you can make whatever edits are necessary. Then you save the changes using the original application's File menu, and those changes are reflected in your Word document.

OLE has given rise to the *compound document,* where you use Word to create your basic document and include text, graphics, video, or sound created in other applications. This topic is sophisticated and complex, but the elements of OLE are actually quite easy to use and offer little chance of error. All that can happen is you don't embed or link the object correctly and you must try again.

For more on embedding, see **Inserting Objects.** For more on linking, see **Linking.**

For a lot more on OLE, see *Word For Windows 6 For Dummies.*

# Opening Files

Opens existing documents. Opening a file in Word means that you want to retrieve an existing document, not create a new one.

## For mouse maniacs

Click the File Open button on the Standard toolbar to display the Open dialog box.

## Opening a file

1. Choose File⇨Open to display the Open dialog box.

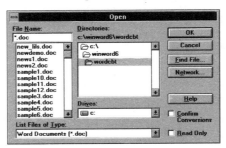

2. Choose the file you want from the list in the File Name box. If you know that you are in the correct directory and you can't see the file you want, you may have to change the type of file (see the next step).

3. By default, Word looks only for document files. These files are indicated by the \*.doc in the File Name box. If the file you want has a different extension, you must change the default. Either type the extension you want directly (**\*.txt**, **\*.\***, and so on) or click in the List Files of Type box to see the types of files you can search for. To see all files in a directory, click the List Files of Type box and choose All Files.

4. To change directories, use the Directories box. To move to a higher or lower level directory, just double-click in that directory. To see other directories on the same drive, double-click in the root directory. When you choose a directory, the files in that directory are displayed in the File Name box.

5. To change drives, click in the Drives box and choose another drive.

6. If you're not sure where the file you want is located, click the Find File button to open the File Find dialog box.

7. If you want to open a file created in another application and you want to confirm its conversion to Word, enable the Confirm Conversions option. If you don't enable this option, Word opens the file without notifying you.

8. To open a file as read-only, enable the <u>R</u>ead Only option. Enabling this option means that you cannot make any changes to the file; you can only view it.

## More stuff

You can choose to open more than one file at a time. If you want to choose a group of consecutive files, click once on the first file in the File <u>N</u>ame box, press Shift, and click once on the last file in the list. All the files in between are also selected. If you want to open a group of nonconsecutive files, click once on the first one and then press Ctrl and click once on each additional file.

For more on finding files, see **File Find.**

For more on file management, see *Word For Windows 6 For Dummies.*

## Options

Lets you set a wide variety of options. Word is a very flexible word processing system. You can enable or disable literally dozens of options. When you combine this capability with the ability to customize keystrokes, menus, and toolbars to your heart's content, listing all the possible combinations of customization and options becomes impossible. You really need to experiment for yourself in this area.

## Setting options

1. Choose <u>T</u>ools⇨<u>O</u>ptions to open the Options dialog box. Note that there are 12 tabs in this dialog box.

2. Click the tab for the category of options you want to set.

3. Click the Help button for help on using that set of options.

## More stuff

Using the <u>T</u>ools menu is not the only way to set options in Word. Many dialog boxes (Print, AutoFormat, and others) have an Options button. If you click the Options button, Word opens the Options dialog box with the specific category selected. Thus you can set options in context even as you work. Where appropriate, this quick reference mentions some of those options.

 For more on setting options in Word, see *Word For Windows 6 For Dummies.*

## Organizer

Lets you copy styles, AutoText entries, macros, and toolbars from one template to another so that you don't have to re-create them. You cannot open the Organizer dialog box directly from a menu. Instead, you must click the Organizer button from the Template dialog box, Style dialog box, or Macro dialog box. (Interestingly, Microsoft did not include an Organizer button in the AutoText dialog box even though you can copy AutoText entries from one template to another using the Organizer.)

## *Using the Organizer*

1. Choose File⇨Templates to open the Template and Add-Ins dialog box, or Format⇨Style to open the Style dialog box, or Tools⇨Macro to open the Macro dialog box.

2. Click the Organizer button to open the Organizer dialog box.

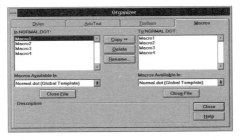

3. Click the tab for the category you want (Styles, AutoText, Toolbars, or Macros).

4. Note the two large boxes. Word labels these boxes depending on your choices. They list items in the chosen document or template based on your choice in step 3. You can copy to either of these boxes from the other. If you choose an item in the box on the left, the Copy button points to the box on the right. If you choose an item in the box on the right, the Copy button points to the box on the left. The items listed in the boxes depend on the document or template listed in the Macros Available In boxes underneath.

5. To change the listed template or document in either Macros Available In box, click the Close File button. This clears both the Macros Available In box and the list of items in the larger box above. The Close File button becomes the Open File button.

6. Click the Open File button to display the Open dialog box. Choose another file or template and click OK. The new template or document is listed in the Macros Available In box, and the items in that document or template are listed in the box above.

7. To delete an item, select it and click the Delete button.

8. To rename an item, select it and click the Rename button. This opens the Rename dialog box, where you can rename the selected item.

9. To copy from one box to the other, select an item in one of the boxes. Click the Copy button to copy the item to the other box.

## More stuff

This feature is a more difficult to describe than it is to use. The problem with describing it is that the labels of the boxes and the buttons in the Organizer dialog box change according to your actions. The best way to find out how to use this feature is to experiment with it.

## Outline View

Lets you view the structure of your document in an outline. Word's outline view provides some special tools to help you quickly view and reorganize even large documents. When you work in outline view, Word displays the Outline toolbar. You can use the buttons on this toolbar to collapse and expand text under headings, move large blocks of material quickly and accurately, generate a table of contents from your headings, and automatically format the headings in your document. After you become familiar with using Word's outline view, you'll wonder how you ever got along without it.

In outline view, *promoting* means changing the selection to a higher heading level; *demoting* means changing the selection to a lower heading level. Word applies its built-in heading levels automatically. You can change body text to headings and headings to body text quickly and easily.

Perhaps one of the nicest features of using the outline view is the ability to collapse all the text under a heading and then move that heading to a different position in the document. The collapsed text moves with the heading. This feature practically eliminates the potential for error when you reorganize the document.

## For mouse maniacs

To switch to outline view quickly, click the Outline View button located on the horizontal scroll bar at the bottom of your screen. Then click any of the outline buttons to perform the indicated action. Outline view is tailor-made for mouse maniacs.

## Switching to outline view

Switching to outline view is simple. Just choose View⇨Outline. To switch back to normal view, choose View⇨Normal.

## Creating an outline

1. Begin a new document.

2. Switch to outline view.

3. Type a heading. Word automatically formats it with the built-in Heading 1 style.

4. Press Enter and type another heading. Word also formats this heading as Heading 1. You can demote this heading if you wish. See the following table for a list of functions you can perform in outline view.

| To | Keystroke | Click |
|----|-----------|-------|
| Promote heading | Alt+Shift+left arrow | Promote button (left arrow) |
| Demote heading | Alt+Shift+right arrow | Demote button (right arrow) |
| Demote heading to body text | Ctrl+Shift+N | Demote to Body Text button (double-headed arrow) |
| Move heading up in document | Alt+Shift+up arrow | Move Up button (up arrow) |
| Move heading down in document | Alt+Shift+down arrow | Move Down button (down arrow) |
| Expand text under heading | Alt+Shift+plus sign | Expand Text button (plus sign) |

| To | Keystroke | Click |
|---|---|---|
| Collapse text under heading | Alt+Shift+minus sign | Collapse Text button (minus sign) |
| Expand or collapse for specified headings | Alt+Shift+*n*, where *n* is the heading level you want to see. | Number of the heading level you want to expand. Word expands that and all higher levels. |
| Expand or collapse entire outline | Alt+Shift+A or press * on numeric keypad | All button |
| Toggle between all text or just first line of text | Alt+Shift+L | Show First Line Only button |
| Show/hide character formatting | Slash key (/) on numeric keypad | Show Formatting button |

## More stuff

If you have to format a document that someone else created without styles, you can switch to outline view, quickly and easily apply Word's built-in heading styles, and reorganize the document as you wish. If the heading formatting is an issue, just redefine the heading styles to match the formats you need. You can even generate a table of contents based on the heading styles.

The key to using the Outlining feature in Word is using Word's built-in heading styles. When you promote or demote a heading, Word automatically applies one of its heading styles.

## Page Numbers

Lets you insert page numbers that Word automatically updates.

## Inserting page numbers

1. Choose Insert⇨Page Numbers to open the Page Numbers dialog box.

2. Determine where you want to position the page numbers in the Position box. You can choose Top of Page or Bottom of Page (the default).

3. Choose the page number alignment you want in the Alignment box. Your choices are Left, Center, Right, Inside, and Outside. (Inside and Outside are for documents that print on both sides of the page and will be bound.) The Preview box reflects the choices you make.

4. To format the page numbers, click the Format button to open the Page Number Format dialog box. You can select from a variety of numbering formats and options.

## *More stuff*

Page numbers in Word are part of headers and footers. You can also insert page numbers while creating a header or footer. For more on headers and footers, see **Headers and Footers.**

## *Page Orientation and Size*

Lets you set the page orientation and page size for a selection of text, a section, or a document. You can set the page to landscape (wide) or portrait (tall).

## *Selecting page orientation*

1. Select the text or place the insertion point in the section you want to change.

2. Choose File⇨Page Setup to open the Page Setup dialog box and click on the Paper Size tab.

3. To set the paper size, click one of the choices in the Paper Size box. If you want to use a custom size, enter the measurements in the Width and Height boxes.

4. To change the orientation, choose Portrait or Landscape in the Orientation section.

5. Select how much of the document you want to get the changes in the Apply To box.

## Page Setup

Lets you configure margins, paper size, paper source, and page
layout, including vertical alignment and line numbers. Changes
that you make in this dialog box can be applied to a selection of
text, a section, or an entire document. The options in this dialog
box are covered in this guide as separate topics.

## More stuff

For more on headers and footers options, see **Headers and
Footers.** For more on line numbers, see **Line Numbering.** For
more on margins, see **Margins.** For more on page orientation and
size, see **Page Orientation and Size.** For more on paper source,
see **Paper Source.**

For more on page layout in Word, see *Word For Windows 6 For
Dummies.*

## Pagination in Word

Lets you adjust how and when page breaks occur. Word normally
begins a new page when the current page is full. This type of page
break is called a *soft page break.* Soft page breaks in Word are
represented by a faint dotted line that runs across the screen.
You can insert a manual page break whenever you want to break
a page. This type of page break is called a *hard page break.* Hard
page breaks in Word are represented by a darker line with the
words Page Break on the line. If you insert a hard page break,
Word readjusts the soft page breaks that follow.

By default, background repagination is enabled in Word. This
means that Word repaginates the document whenever you pause.
You can turn background repagination off in normal and outline
views, but background repagination is always on in print preview
and page layout view (because these views always show an entire
page). You can also specify that lines in a paragraph and selected
paragraphs be kept together on one page and that certain
paragraphs start a page. Word also lets you specify whether
widow and orphan lines (single lines at the tops and bottoms of a
page) are permitted. Other factors that affect pagination include
whether hidden text and field codes are displayed and whether
you use hyphenation in your document.

# Setting background repagination

1. Switch to normal view. (Remember that background pagination is always on in page layout view and print preview.)

2. Choose Tools⇨Options to open the Options dialog box and click the General tab.

3. Enable the Background Repagination option to have Word repaginate automatically; clear it to turn off background pagination.

# Inserting and removing hard page breaks

To insert a hard page break, position the insertion point where you want the page break and press Ctrl+Enter. To remove a hard page break, select it and press Delete or Backspace.

# Setting orphan and widow control

If you enable widow/orphan control, Word does not print single lines of text at the top or bottom of a page.

1. Choose Format⇨Paragraph to open the Paragraph dialog box and click the Text Flow tab.

2. Either clear or enable the Widow/Orphan option.

3. Click OK.

# Printing a paragraph at the top of a page

This option is most commonly applied to titles and section headings.

1. Position the insertion point in the paragraph you want to begin a page.

2. Choose Format⇨Paragraph to open the Paragraph dialog box and click the Text Flow tab.

3. Enable the Page Break Before option under Pagination.

4. Click OK.

## *More stuff*

For more on pagination and lines and paragraphs, see **Keeping Lines and Paragraphs Together.**

## *Paper Source*

Lets you specify which tray to print from and whether the printer should feed from a different source for the first page. You can specify a different paper source for each section in your document.

### *Specifying the paper source when printing*

1. If you want to specify a paper source for the first page of a section or a single section, position the insertion point in that section. If you want to specify a paper source for several sections, either choose them or perform this procedure several times.

2. Choose Tools➪Options to open the Options dialog box and click the Print tab (or choose File➪Print and click the Options button).

3. Choose the print option you want in the Default Tray box.

4. Click OK.

### *Specifying a different source for the first page of each section*

1. Choose File➪Page Setup to open the Page Setup dialog box and click the Paper Source tab.

2. Choose the trays you want to use in the First Page and the Other Pages boxes.

3. Select how much of the document you want to apply these changes to in the Apply To box. The Preview box shows the results of the options you choose.

4. Click OK.

## Paragraph Spacing

Lets you specify the exact amount of space above and below selected paragraphs. You can, of course, just press Enter to create space after a paragraph, but using paragraph spacing lets you be far more precise about the amount of space above and below selected paragraphs.

### For keyboard kut-ups

To insert 12 points (12 points equals one line of text) of spacing above a paragraph, place the insertion point in the paragraph and press

### Adjusting paragraph spacing

1. Choose Format⇨Paragraph to open the Paragraph dialog box.

2. Click the Indents and Spacing tab.

3. To add spacing above a paragraph, enter a value in the Spacing Before box. To add spacing below a paragraph, enter a value in the Spacing After box. You can click the arrows to use Word's default increment, or you can type a value directly in the box.

4. Click OK.

### More stuff

Note that the values in the spacing boxes are in points where 12 points equals one line of text. Because you can enter any value, you can be precise about the amount of spacing above and below the selected paragraphs.

## Paste Special

Lets you paste, embed, or link the contents of the Clipboard. What you do is copy information to the Clipboard and then place the insertion point where you want to insert the contents of the

Clipboard. Then choose one of the options from the Paste Special dialog box to embed, link, or just plain copy the Clipboard contents.

## Using Paste Special

1. Open the application or document that has the object or information you want to copy.

2. Select the information or object and copy it to the Clipboard.

3. Switch to your Word document.

4. Place the insertion point where you want to insert the object.

5. Choose Edit⇨Paste Special to open the Paste Special dialog box.

6. Choose the option you want and click OK.

## More stuff

For more on this topic, see **OLE, Insert Object,** and **Linking.**

## Pasting

Inserts the contents of the Clipboard to the current position in your document but doesn't embed or create links.

## For keyboard kut-ups

To paste text or graphics, place the insertion point where you want to insert the information; then press

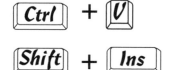

or

## For mouse maniacs

Place the insertion point where you want and then click on the Paste button on the Standard toolbar.

## More stuff

Cutting, copying, and pasting are really three parts of the same operation. For more on this, see **Cutting** and **Copying.**

*Print Preview*

Lets you preview a document before you print it. Word's Print Preview feature lets you view multiple pages. You can use the Print Preview toolbar to edit the document before you print it.

## For keyboard kut-ups

To toggle between print preview and normal view, press

## Opening and closing print preview

1. Position the insertion point where you want to begin previewing your document.

2. Choose File⇨Print Preview.

3. To close print preview, click the Close button.

## Editing in print preview

1. Open print preview.

2. Note that the mouse pointer becomes a magnifier. Clicking toggles you between zooming in and out of your document. To edit in print preview, disable the zooming function of the pointer by clicking the Magnifier button.

3. Use the Print Preview toolbar to perform the function you want.

## More stuff

You can perform editing actions in print preview, including changing the margins. For more on changing margins in print preview, see **Margins.**

## Printing

Lets you print all or part of your document. Besides printing the document, you can also select various elements of the document to print, such as hidden text and field text.

## For keyboard kut-ups

To print the entire document, press

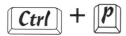

## For mouse maniacs

Click the print button on the Standard toolbar. This shortcut prints the entire document. If you want to select options or print part of the document, you must use the menu.

## Printing your document

1. Choose File⇨Print to open the Print dialog box.

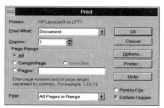

2. Select the options you want to print.
3. Click OK to begin printing.

## Setting more print options

The Print Options dialog box gives you many more printing options.

1. Open the Print Options dialog box either by choosing File⇨Print and clicking the Print Options button or by choosing Tools⇨Options and clicking the Print tab.

2. Select the options you want.

3. Click OK.

## Protecting Documents

Lets you set passwords for documents so that others cannot change them.

## Setting document protection

1. Choose Tools⇨Protect Document to open the Protect Document dialog box.

2. Select the options you want.

3. Type your password in the Password box. It can be up to 15 characters long and can include letters, numbers, symbols, and spaces. The password is case-sensitive, so you have to use the same combination of upper- and lowercase letters. You must later use the same password whenever you want to remove protection from the document. When you enter the password, Word prompts you to enter it a second time. If you don't type it exactly the same way the second time, the document is not password protected.

## More stuff

Don't forget your password. You won't be able to unprotect the document. Even if you do a Save As, the new file will also be password protected.

## Repeat Last Action

Lets you repeat your last action, whatever it was. This feature is little-known but quite useful and adds real quality of life to using Word.

## For keyboard kut-ups

To repeat your last action, press

## Repeating your last action

To repeat whatever your last action was, choose Edit⇔Repeat. The word *Repeat* is followed by whatever the last action was.

## More stuff

In Word, the last action means the last action. For example, if you selected text and formatted it as bold and italic, pressing F4 would repeat only the italicizing on your next selection. However, if you use the Format Font dialog box, you can apply any number of font formats. Word repeats them all when you press F4 because your last action took place in the dialog box.

---

## Revisions

Lets you track any revisions made to your document.

## Marking revisions

When you specify that you want to mark revisions, Word marks each changed and new paragraph with a revision bar in the margin, underlines new text, and displays deleted text as strikethrough. Word also indicates who made changes and when the changes were made.

1. Choose Tools⇔Revisions to open the Revisions dialog box.

2. To mark revisions to your document, enable the Mark Revisions While Editing option.

3. To display the revisions as you modify the document, enable the Show Revisions on Screen option.

4. To print the revision marks with the document, enable the Show Revisions in Printed Document option.

5. If you want to customize how Word displays the revisions, click the Options button to open the Revisions Options dialog box.

## Reviewing revisions

Word lets you accept or reject all the revisions at once, or you can review each revision individually and accept, reject, or ignore it.

1. Choose Tools⇨Revisions to open the Revisions dialog box.

2. To accept or reject all the revisions, click the appropriate button. Word asks you to confirm your selection.

3. Click the Review button to open the Review Revisions dialog box.

4. Click one of the Find buttons to move to the next or previous revision.

5. To move to the next revision automatically, enable the Find Next After Accept/Reject option.

6. To hide the revision marks as you review, click the Hide Marks button. The button changes to the Show Marks button so that you can display the revision marks again.

7. To accept a revision, click the Accept button. Word removes the revision mark.

8. To reject a revision, click the Reject button. Word removes the revision mark.

9. To undo the last decision you made, click the Undo Last button.

## More stuff

You can also compare two versions of the same document. For more on this, see **Comparing Document Versions.**

## Rulers

Lets you change margins and some paragraph formats, set tabs, and resize table columns. Word has two rulers: the horizontal ruler and the vertical ruler. You can see the vertical ruler only in page layout view and in print preview. Neither ruler is visible in outline view.

## Changing the measuring system on the rulers

The default measuring system that Word uses for the rulers is inches. However, you can specify points, picas, or centimeters instead.

1. Choose <u>T</u>ools➪<u>O</u>ptions to open the Options dialog box; then click the General tab.

2. Click once in the <u>M</u>easurement Units box to see the measuring options.

3. Select the measurement system you want and click OK. The rulers now display measurements in that system.

You can use the rulers to accomplish graphically certain formatting tasks. The use of the ruler to do these things is covered under the specific topic. For example, to use the ruler to set indents, see **Indenting.**

---

## Saving

Saves a document to disk. Perhaps the single most frustrating thing about using computers is to lose a bunch of work because you haven't saved it. *Saving* means making a permanent record of what you're doing, regardless of the software you use. When you save a document for the first time, you give it a filename and specify a location for the file. Each time you save the file subsequently, you write the changes you make to disk. You can also use the Save As command to save an existing file in a different format, to a new location, or under a different name (or any combination of these options). Word also has an AutoSave feature, which you can use to protect yourself from accidental loss of data.

## For keyboard kut-ups

To save the current file, press

$$\boxed{Shift} + \boxed{F12}$$

or

$$\boxed{Alt} + \boxed{Shift} + \boxed{F12}$$

or

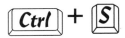

To use the Save As command, press

## For mouse maniacs

Click the Save button on the Standard toolbar to save the current file.

## Saving a document for the first time

1. Choose File⇨Save to open the Save As dialog box.

2. Type the name you want to give your document under File Name. The name must not be more than 8 letters or numbers and can contain no spaces. If you don't add an extension (the characters after the period), Word automatically gives it the DOC extension.

3. Choose the directory where you want to store the file in the Directories box.

4. To change drives, click in the Drives box to see the available drives.

5. If you want to save the file in a format other than Word for Windows 6, click in the Save File As Type box to see the available formats. Choose the format you want.

6. Click OK to save the file. Word displays the new name in the title bar of the Word window.

## Using File Save As

When you save a file for the first time, you give it a name and location. Each time you save that file subsequently, no dialog box appears. Instead, Word writes the changes to the disk so that they become a permanent part of that file. However, occasionally, you might want to save an existing file with a different name, in a different location, or in a different format. File Save As gives you the ability to perform any or all of these options. When you use the File Save As command on an existing file, you create a new file. Word closes the original file and stores it in its original location.

1. Choose File⇨Save As to open the Save As dialog box. Word displays the current file name in the File Name box.

2. To create a new file with a different name, type the new name in the File Name box.

3. To create a new file in a different location, change the drive and directory (or either one).

4. To create a new file with a different file format, choose the format from the Save File as Type box.

5. Click OK to create the new file. Word closes the original and stores it in its original location. If you gave the file a new name, that name is displayed in the title bar. The new file is an exact copy of the original, except for its name, location, or file format (depending on what you changed). Changes you make to the new file have no effect on the original, as they are now two separate and distinct files.

## Using AutoSave

Word's AutoSave feature is really a disaster prevention feature because it doesn't permanently save changes to your file. The decision whether or not to save changes to your file is entirely yours. Instead, Word creates a temporary file that it updates periodically while you work. You specify how often Word performs the AutoSave.

When you exit Word normally at the end of a work session, you either save or discard the changes you've made during the session. At that point, Word erases the temp file because it's no longer needed.

However, if disaster strikes (such as a power failure), Word keeps the temp file. The very next time you open Word, the AutoSave feature displays all the temp files it saved and lets you decide whether or not to save them. So, if you had set AutoSave to update the temp file every 10 minutes, for example, you can't have lost more than 10 minutes worth of work.

You can see that this feature is important. Enabling AutoSave is in your best interests.

1. Choose Tools⇨Options and click the Save tab to open the Save Options dialog box. (You can also open this dialog box by choosing File⇨Save As and then clicking the Options button.)

2. Enable the Automatic Save option.

3. Set the interval for automatic saves. The default is 10 minutes.

4. Click OK to enable the AutoSave feature.

## More stuff

When AutoSave displays a recovered file after an abnormal exit, Word displays the filename followed by the word RECOVERED in the title bar.

For more on saving files, see *Word For Windows 6 For Dummies*.

## Sections

Lets you change certain page formatting options for parts of your document. When you create a document, it consists of a single section. Any page formatting (margins, headers/footers, paper size, page numbering, and so on) is applied to the entire document. However, if you want to change page formatting for certain parts of the document, you must create sections.

## Inserting a section break

Section breaks are displayed as double-dotted lines and are labeled End of Section.

1. Position the insertion point where you want to begin the new section.

2. Choose Insert⇨Break to open the Break dialog box.

3. Under Section Breaks, choose where you want the section break to occur. Next Page means the section break begins a new page. Continuous means the section break follows the previous section without inserting a page break. Even Page starts the section break at the next even-numbered page; Odd Page starts the section break at the next odd-numbered page. (Even Pages and Odd Pages are usually used for chapters that begin on even- or odd-numbered pages.)

To delete a section break, select it and press Backspace or Delete.

## More stuff

 When you delete a section break, you also delete any section formatting for the text above the deleted section break. That text becomes part of the next section and uses that section's formatting.

 Some formats that require sections insert the necessary section breaks automatically, depending on how you apply the formatting. For example, you might need to format part of your document with multiple newspaper-style columns. You can insert section breaks above and below the text to be formatted with columns and then apply the column formatting, or you can select the text and apply the column formatting to have Word automatically insert the necessary section breaks.

 Formatting elements that require their own sections are covered separately under those topics in this guide.

## Selecting

Highlights a portion of your document. Selecting, also known as highlighting or blocking, is a fundamental principle of working in Word for Windows. First, you select what you want to work on; then you work on it. The table that follows lists some shortcut mouse methods for selecting text.

| To select | Do this |
|---|---|
| Any item or text | Drag over what you want to select. |
| A word | Double-click the word. |
| A line of text | Position the pointer to the left of the line until it becomes an arrow pointing upper right and then click. |
| Multiple lines | Select a line and drag over the additional lines. |
| A sentence | Click anywhere in the sentence while pressing Ctrl. |
| A paragraph | Triple-click anywhere in the paragraph. |
| The entire document | Position the pointer to the left of any part of the document until the pointer becomes an arrow pointing upper right; then press Ctrl and click. |

## *Shortcut Menus*

Displays a context-sensitive shortcut menu using the mouse. Move the pointer to text or over a toolbar and press the right button to see the shortcut menu. Items on the menu are appropriate for whatever you pointed at.

## *Sorting*

Sorts rows in tables, lists, and paragraphs. You can sort alphabetically, numerically, or by date order.

### *Sorting text*

1. Select the text you want to sort. Word sorts text paragraph by paragraph. If you don't select text to sort, Word selects the entire document for sorting.

2. Choose Table⇨Sort Text to open the Sort Text dialog box.

3. Choose the options you want.

4. Click OK to sort the selected text.

### *More stuff*

Sorting is performed mostly in tables. For more on tables, see **Tables.**

## *Spelling Checker*

Spell checks a selection of text or the entire document. Word's spell checker also catches capitalization errors and instances where you type a word twice in a row.

# For keyboard kut-ups

To begin a spelling check, press

# For mouse maniacs

To begin a spelling check, click the Spelling button on the Standard toolbar.

# Using the spell checker

1. Choose Tools⇨Spelling to begin the spelling check.

2. For each word not found in the dictionary, Word displays the Spelling dialog box. Choose the option you want, and the spelling check continues until Word has completed checking the entire document (or whatever portion of the document you selected).

3. If, during the spelling check, you want to make a change to the document, you can make the change without closing the dialog box. After you make the change, you can resume the spelling check by clicking the Start button.

# Setting options

1. Choose Tools⇨Options to open the Options dialog box; then click the Spelling tab. (Or you can click the Options button in the Spelling dialog box.)

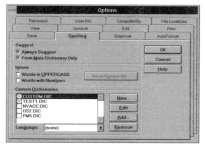

2. Choose the options you want.

## Creating a custom dictionary

Creating custom dictionaries is easy and desirable. When you create a custom dictionary, any words you add are added only to that dictionary. You can add terms specific to specialized documents, names, titles, whatever you like. When you use the custom dictionary, the spelling checker does not stop on words you added to that dictionary. The main dictionary and other custom dictionaries remain unchanged.

## More stuff

You can quickly add a lot of words to a custom dictionary from the Spelling Options dialog box. Choose the dictionary and click the Edit button to open the dictionary as a Word document. Then type the words you want to add. Press Enter after you type each word. When you finish, save and close the file as you would any Word document. The list you typed is added to the custom dictionary, and the spelling checker no longer stops on those words when you use that dictionary.

Word's grammar checker incorporates the spelling checker when you use it.

While spelling checkers are wonderful tools and should be used as often as you like, they have some drawbacks. For one thing, a spelling check does not catch a word that is spelled correctly but used incorrectly (that is, John has two much money). (Actually, this sentence is a good candidate for the grammar checker.) For another reason, if you inadvertently add a misspelled word to the dictionary, the spelling checker won't catch that word until you remove it.

## Spike

Lets you remove multiple items from different locations and documents and insert them all in another location or document. The Spike is a multiple cut-and-paste tool; it works like the old editor's spike that collected pieces of paper until the editor had time to get to them. Items you add to the Spike are added in order so that, when you paste the contents of the Spike, the items appear in the same order as you added them. The Spike is a tool made to order for you keyboard kut-ups.

## Using the Spike

To cut something out of your document and add it to the Spike, select it and press

| Ctrl | + | F3 |

To paste the contents of the Spike and clear it at the same time, press

| Ctrl | + | Shift | + | F3 |

To paste the contents of the Spike without clearing it, type **spike** and press

| Alt | + | Ctrl | + | V |

---

### Splitting a Window

Lets you split your document window into two horizontal parts called *panes.* The panes scroll independently of each other so that you can work on different parts of the document at the same time or display different views at the same time.

## Splitting the document window

1. Choose <u>W</u>indow⇨S<u>p</u>lit. Your mouse pointer becomes attached to a line running across the screen.

2. Move the mouse pointer with the line attached to the position where you want the split to occur.

3. Click the left mouse button once. The document window splits into two panes, each with its own ruler. Just click in the one you want to work in to make it active.

To remove the split, simply choose <u>W</u>indow⇨Remove S<u>p</u>lit.

# Style Gallery

Lets you use styles from a different template. The Style Gallery lets you preview your document as it would look with styles from another template. If you decide to use the styles from another template, the Style Gallery copies all the styles from that template into the current one. It does not replace the current template with the one you chose in the Style Gallery.

## Using the Style Gallery

1. Choose Format⇨Style Gallery to open the Style Gallery dialog box.

2. Choose the template you want to use in the Template box.

3. To display the active document as it will look with styles from the selected template, choose Document in the Preview area.

4. To display a sample document formatted with styles from the selected template, choose Example in the Preview area.

5. To display a list of the styles in the selected template with sample text formatted using the styles, choose Style Samples in the Preview area.

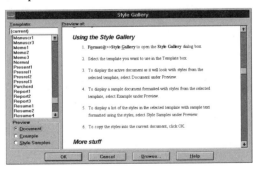

6. To copy the styles into the current document, click OK.

## More stuff

Even though the Style Gallery can quickly add a bunch of styles to the current template, there is a drawback. If one of the styles from the other template has the same name as a style in the current template, the incoming style overwrites the current style. The result is unwanted change, especially if the style in question is used frequently throughout the document.

If you don't like the way your document looks after you choose another template, click the Undo button.

## Styles

Lets you assign and update formatting quickly and easily. Using styles is one of the keys to getting the most out of Word (or any major word processing program). Basically, a style is a collection of formats. Instead of applying the formatting directly to text, you apply the style. This makes applying formatting easier and ensures uniformity of formatting. Later, if you need to change some of the formatting, you can change the style instead. Then, all the text that has that style applied gets the new formatting automatically.

Word has two types of styles: *paragraph* and *character*. A paragraph style means that the formatting defined in the style is applied to the entire paragraph; a character style means that the formatting defined in the style is applied to selected characters. Paragraph styles can include font formatting, paragraph formatting, tab formatting, border formatting, language formatting, frame formatting, and numbering formatting. Character styles include only font formatting and language formatting. You can define styles to have any or all of these formatting elements.

Word provides a default style for many elements of a document. For example, when you begin a new document, Word automatically applies the Normal style, which is its built-in style for body text. So you really use styles in Word whether you know it or not. Word also automatically applies styles to certain other elements (headers and footers, indexes, tables of contents, captions, and so on). The table that follows lists the style that Word applies automatically. You can change the definition of any of these default styles.

Direct formatting always overrides a style so that you or anyone else can apply whatever formatting is necessary to any part of a document, whether it has been assigned a style or not. The definition of the style won't change unless you specifically make it change.

When you create a style, that style is included in the document. If you want it to be available to other new documents based on the template the current document is using, you can add the style to the template. Then every new document based on that template will also have that style available. If you want to get a style from a different document or template, you can copy it using the Organizer.

As with so many features in Word, there are several ways to create and modify styles. The easiest method is to use example text, but you can also use the Style dialog box. If you are new to styles, try creating and editing a style from example text. You will be surprised at how simple it is and what a powerful tool it is.

## *Creating a style from example text*

This method creates paragraph styles. If you want to create a character style, use the Style dialog box instead.

1. Select the paragraph that has the formatting you want to save as a style. If necessary, create such a paragraph by formatting it appropriately.

2. Click in the Style box on the Formatting toolbar to choose whatever is currently in the box.

3. Delete the current name.

4. Type a name for the new style.

5. Press Enter. That's it. You now have a new style that you can apply to other paragraphs.

Word defines the style you create in this manner to have the font, size, and other character formats of the first character of the selected text.

## *Creating a style using the Style command*

1. Choose Format⇨Style to open the Style dialog box.

2. Click the New button to open the New Style dialog box.

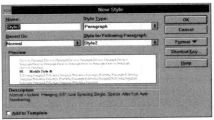

3. Type a name for the new style in the <u>N</u>ame box.

4. Choose the type of style you want in the Style <u>T</u>ype box. The default is a Paragraph style.

5. Choose a current style to <u>b</u>ase the new style on. By default, Word bases a new style on the style applied to the selected paragraph. When you base a new style on an existing style, the new style begins with the formats of the based-on style.

6. Click the <u>F</u>ormat button to see a list of format categories. Choose the format category (font, paragraph, and so on) that you want to open the appropriate dialog box, where you can choose the specific formats you want. When you close the format dialog box, you return to the New Style dialog box so that you can choose another category of formatting to include in the new style.

7. To create a shortcut keystroke for applying the style, click the Shortcut <u>K</u>ey button to open the Customize dialog box.

8. When you have included all the formats you want, click OK to create the style.

## Applying a style

You can apply a style by using the Style dialog box, but using the Formatting toolbar is much quicker and easier.

1. Select the text you want to have a style. If you want to apply a character style to specific text, you must select that text. The insertion point must be in a paragraph to apply a paragraph style.

2. Click the down arrow to the right of the Style box on the Formatting toolbar to see the list of current styles. Paragraph styles are bolded; character styles are not bolded.

3. Choose the style. Word applies the formatting immediately to whatever you selected.

You can quickly apply the same style to several items. Follow the preceding steps to apply the style the first time. Then choose the next item to get the style and press F4 (the repeat key). Continue choosing and pressing F4 until you've applied the style everywhere you want.

You can also use a shortcut keystroke to apply a style. For more on shortcut keystrokes, see **Keyboard Shortcuts.**

## Removing character styles

You cannot remove a paragraph style; instead, you must assign another style. However, you can remove a character style. To remove a character style, select the text that has the character style and press Ctrl+spacebar.

## Modifying a style's formats using example text

1. Select the item that is formatted with the style you want to change. If you want to change a character style, select at least one character that uses that style.

2. Modify the formatting of whatever you selected as desired.

3. Click on the style name in the Style box on the Formatting toolbar and then press Enter.

4. Word asks you if you want to redefine the style. Click OK. The new formats are immediately applied to any part of the document formatted with that style.

## Modifying a style's formats using the Style dialog box

You can use this procedure to modify the default styles that Word uses. For example, you might want to change the Envelope Address style.

1. Choose Format⇨Style to open the Style dialog box.

2. Choose the style you want to modify in the Styles box. If you don't see the style you want, click in the List box to see more categories of styles.

3. Click the Modify button to open the Modify dialog box.

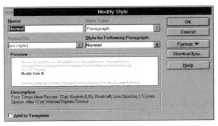

4. To modify the style, click the Format button to choose a category of formatting and open the appropriate dialog box.

5. To use the modified style in new documents based on the current template, enable the Add To Template option at the bottom of the dialog box.

6. Click OK to redefine the style.

## Using styles and templates

You make styles available to other documents by adding the style to a template. A *template* is a special kind of document that acts as a blueprint for other documents. When you create a new file based on a template, Word opens a copy of that template. The copy includes any text from the template itself, and all styles, macros, AutoText entries, toolbars, and customized menu and keystroke shortcuts. For more on templates, see **Templates.**

## Copying styles to other documents and templates

You can copy styles from one document or template to another so you don't have to create the same style again.

1. Choose Format⇨Style to open the Style dialog box.
2. Click the Organizer button to open the Organizer dialog box.
3. Click the Styles tab.
4. Copy the styles.
5. Click Close.

For more on using the Organizer, see **Organizer.**

## Deleting a style

When you delete a paragraph style, Word assigns the Normal style to any paragraphs that were formatted with the deleted style.

1. Choose Format⇨Style to open the Style dialog box.
2. Choose the style you want to delete in the Styles box.
3. Click the Delete button to delete the style. Word displays a confirmation message.
4. Click OK to confirm.
5. Click Close.

## Renaming a style

1. Choose Format⇨Style to open the Style dialog box.
2. Choose the style you want to rename in the Styles box.
3. Click the Modify button to open the Modify Styles dialog box.
4. Type the new name for the style in the Name box.
5. Click OK to return to the Style dialog box; then click Close to return to your document.

## Displaying style names as you work

You can display the names of the styles applied to text as you work. If you display the style names, you can see them only in normal or page layout view.

1. Choose Tools⇨Options and then click the View tab to open the View Options dialog box.

2. To display style names, set the Style Area Width value to 0.5. (You can set other values, but 0.5 usually suffices.)

3. Click OK. Your Word screen is vertically split, with the applied style names showing on the left.

4. To close the Style Area, drag the vertical line off the screen to the left or set the Style Area Width in the View Options dialog box to zero.

## Printing the styles in your document

You can print a list of all the styles available in the current document and their definitions.

1. Choose File⇨Print to open the Print dialog box.

2. Click once in the Print What box to display the items you can print instead of the document itself.

3. Choose Styles.

4. Click OK.

## More stuff

You can base a group of related styles on a single base style so that changes made to the base style affect the related styles as well.

 There are a number of subtleties and facets to styles that cannot be covered in this guide. For more on styles, see *Word For Windows 6 For Dummies.*

## Summary Information

Adds extra information that you can later use to find documents. Summary information can be added any time, or you can specify that Word prompt you for summary information each time you first save a new file. You can add a title, author, subject, and keyword information on a file. You can use Word's Find File feature to search for that information if you cannot locate the file later. The Summary Information dialog box allows you to open the Statistics window, where you can see a list of statistics about your document.

## Setting User Information to prompt automatically

1. Choose <u>T</u>ools⇨<u>O</u>ptions and then click the Save tab to open the Save Options dialog box.

2. Enable the Prompt For Summary Info option under Save Options; then click OK.

## Viewing and editing summary information

1. Choose <u>F</u>ile⇨Summary <u>I</u>nfo to open the Summary Information dialog box.

2. To edit the information, make changes in the <u>T</u>itle, <u>S</u>ubject, <u>A</u>uthor, <u>K</u>eywords, and <u>C</u>omments boxes.

3. Click OK.

## Viewing document statistics

1. Choose <u>F</u>ile⇨Summary <u>I</u>nfo to open the Summary Information dialog box.

2. Click the Stat<u>i</u>stics button to open the Statistics window.

3. When you finish viewing the statistics, click Close to return to the Summary Information dialog box.

## Searching for documents by using summary info

1. Choose <u>F</u>ile⇨<u>F</u>ind File to open the Find File dialog box.

2. Click the <u>S</u>earch button to open the Search dialog box.

3. Click the <u>A</u>dvanced Search button to open the Advanced Search dialog box.

4. Click the <u>S</u>ummary tab.

5. Enter the information you want Word to search for.

6. Click OK to begin the search.

## More stuff

Summary information can be a helpful tool, but it has its drawbacks. Perhaps the major drawback is that you can easily forget what summary information you entered about a file that's months or years old when you need to search for it. And if you enter a lot of summary information in the Advanced Search dialog box, you can decrease your chances of finding the file, because a single misspelling of a keyword causes Word to bypass the file.

On the other hand, the Find File dialog box lets you view selected files by content, by file info, or by summary information. It can be interesting and instructive to see the summary information on a selected file.

## Symbols

Insert symbols and special characters you cannot type from the keyboard. Some examples of such special characters are registration symbols, trademark symbols, en and em dashes, and bullets. (Actually, Word makes typing the most common symbols easy by giving them keystrokes, and Word handles bullets and numbers comprehensively.) Most fonts have character sets, which contain symbols not found on the keyboard. Word makes inserting any symbol from an installed font easy.

## For keyboard kut-ups

If you're a keyboard kut-up, Word lets you insert the most common special characters with ease. The table that follows lists some special characters and their keystroke combinations.

| Special Character | Keystroke |
| --- | --- |
| — (Em Dash) | Alt+Ctrl+hyphen (on the numeric keypad only) |
| – (En Dash) | Ctrl+hyphen (on the numeric keypad only) |
| - (Nonbreaking Hyphen) | Ctrl+underscore |
| ⌐ (Optional Hyphen - this character can be seen only if the Show/Hide button is enabled) | Ctrl+hyphen |
| ₀ (Nonbreaking space - this character can be seen only if the Show/Hide button is enabled) | Ctrl+Shift+spacebar |

| Special Character | Keystroke |
|---|---|
| © (Copyright symbol) | Alt+Ctrl+C |
| ® (Registration symbol) | Alt+Ctrl+R |
| ™ (Trademark symbol) | Alt+Ctrl+T |
| …(Ellipsis) | Alt+Ctrl+period |

## Inserting a symbol

1. Position the insertion point where you want to insert the symbol.

2. Choose Insert⇨Symbol to open the Symbol dialog box.

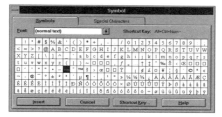

3. Click on the Symbols tab.

4. To see the symbols available to a particular font, choose that font in the Font box. The symbols displayed in the matrix change, depending on the font you choose. When you click on a box in the matrix, Word magnifies that selection so that you can see it better.

5. Be sure to check the Symbol font. Also, if you have Zapf Dingbats or any of the Wingding fonts installed, check them in the Font box for unusual symbols. Word lists the shortcut keystroke for some symbols.

6. To see a list of special characters that you can insert, click the Special Characters tab.

7. To assign a shortcut keystroke to a particular symbol, choose the symbol and click the Shortcut Key button to open the Customize dialog box. (For more on assigning shortcut keystrokes, see **Keyboard Shortcuts.**)

8. To insert a chosen symbol in your document, click the Insert button.

## More stuff

If you are a long time computer user, you may remember that in earlier days you could insert special characters by making sure the Num Lock light is on, pressing Alt and typing a number code on the numeric keypad. Well, you can still do this. The approaches described above are just an automated way of doing the same thing. The benefit to using Word's approach is that you don't need to remember codes or keep a list of codes.

## Table of Authorities

Lists where citations occur in legal documents. A *citation* is a reference to case law, statutes, rules, and so on. Tables of Authorities are specialized documents that are frequently used by those involved in the law business, but hardly, if ever, by anyone else. A table of authorities takes three basic steps: marking or typing the entries, choosing a format, and compiling the table.

## *Marking citations*

When you mark a citation, Word inserts a field that is formatted as hidden, so you need to be able to view hidden text to see the citation marks. For more on fields, see **Fields;** for more on hidden text, see **Hidden Text.**

There are long citations and short citations in a table of authorities. The first instance of a particular citation should be the long citation. Later additional references to that citation are short. In other words, the first citation contains all the pertinent data.

1. Select the citation you want to mark.

2. Press Alt+Shift+I to open the Mark Citation dialog box. The selected text appears in both the Selected Text box and the Short Citation box.

3. Edit and format the entry in the Selected Text box for the long citation as you want it to appear in the Table of Authorities. You can use only shortcut keys (Ctrl+B for Bold, Ctrl+I for Italic, Ctrl+U for Underline) to apply character formatting.

4. Choose the appropriate category in the Category box.

5. Edit the text in the Short Citation box so that it matches the short citation you want Word to search for in the document.

6. To mark the citation, click the Mark button. The dialog box remains open for you to mark other citations.

7. To mark all instances of long and short citations that match what you entered in the Short Citation and Long Citation boxes, click the Mark All button. The dialog box remains open for you to mark other citations.

8. To have Word search for the next citation, click the Next Citation button. Word searches for the next occurrence of text commonly found in citations, such as *in re* or *v.*

9. Select the text for the next citation and repeat steps 3 through 8.

10. When you finish marking the citations, click the Close button.

## Modifying citation categories

Each citation is marked with a category. You can change any of Word's default categories, and you can add up to 8 of your own. A table of authorities can contain up to 16 categories.

1. In the Mark Citation dialog box, click the Category button to open the Edit Category dialog box.

2. To replace an existing category, choose the name you want to replace.

3. To add a new category, choose one of the numbers from 8 to 16 under Category.

4. Type the name of the new category in the Replace With box.

5. Click the Replace button.

6. Click OK to return to the Mark Citation dialog box.

## Formatting and compiling the table of authorities

1. Position the insertion point where you want the table of authorities.

2. Choose Insert⇨Index And Tables to open the Index and Tables dialog box.

3. Click the Table of Authorities tab.

4. Choose the category you want to compile in the Category box. To compile all the categories, choose All.

5. To replace five or more page references to the same authority with *passim,* enable the Use Passim option.

6. Enable the Keep Original Formatting option to retain the formatting of the citation as it appears in the document.

7. To insert tab leader characters between the entries and the page numbers, choose the tab leader character in the Tab Leader box.

8. Choose the format you want for the table in the Formats box.

9. Click OK to close the dialog box and compile the table.

## More stuff

For more on Tables of Authority, see *Word For Windows 6 For Dummies.*

# Table of Contents

Inserts a table of contents based on either heading levels or fields that you insert.

You might want to consider using a master document if you are working on a long document. For more on master documents, see **Master Documents.**

## Creating table of contents entries

The easiest way to create your table of contents is to use Word's built-in heading styles (Heading 1 through Heading 9). You can compile a table of contents directly from the headings. Or you can insert Table Of Contents Entry (TC) fields to create your table of contents.

1. Place the insertion point next to the text you want to include in the table of contents.

2. Choose Insert⇔Field to open the Field dialog box.

3. Choose Index and Tables in the Categories box.

4. Choose TC in the Field Names box.

5. Click OK to insert the TC field.

## Creating a table of contents from heading styles

1. Be sure that the headings in your document are formatted with Word's built-in heading styles.

2. Position the insertion point where you want the table of contents.

3. Choose Insert⇔Index And Tables to open the Index and Tables dialog box.

4. Click the Table of Contents tab.

5. Choose the format you want from the Formats box.

6. To show page numbers in the table of contents, enable the Show Page Numbers option.

7. To specify the heading level you want in the table of contents, enter the number you want to display in the Show Levels box.

8. To right-align the page numbers, enable the Right Align Page Numbers option.

9. To use tab leaders, choose one in the Tab Leaders box.

10. Click OK to create the table of contents.

## Creating a table of contents from fields or other styles

If you are using TC fields to create the table of contents, the fields should all be inserted before using this procedure.

1. Position the insertion point where you want the table of contents.

2. Choose Insert⇨Index And Tables to open the Index and Tables dialog box.

3. Click the Table of Contents tab.

4. Choose the format you want from the Form"ts box.

5. Click the Options button to open the Table of Contents Options dialog box.

6. If you are using styles other than Word's built-in heading styles to create your table of contents, find the styles you are using in the Available Styles box. Use the scroll bar to the right of the blank boxes to scroll.

7. Type a number from 1 to 9 in the TOC Level box to the right of the style name you are using for your headings. The number you type should correspond to the heading level of that style.

8. If you are using TC fields instead of styles for your table of contents, disable the Styles option and enable the Table Entry Fields option.

9. Click OK to close the Table Of Contents Options dialog box and return to the Index And Tables dialog box.

10. Click OK to compile the table of contents.

## *Table of Figures*

Lists figure captions in the order they appear in your document. You can include tables of items such as illustrations, figures, charts, graphs, and other elements. A table of figures usually appears just after a table of contents, at the beginning of a document.

 The easiest way to create a table of figures is to use Word's Caption command to add captions to your figures and other items. When the item has a caption, Word can include it in the table of figures. For more on using captions, see **Captions.**

## *Creating a table of figures*

Creating a table of figures is similar to creating a table of contents.

1. Position the insertion point where you want the table of figures.

2. Choose Insert⇨Index and Tables to open the Index And Tables dialog box.

3. Click the Table of Figures tab.

4. Choose the type of caption label you want to compile in the Caption Label box.

5. Enable the Show Page Numbers option to display page numbers in the table of figures.

6. Enable the Include Label and Number option to include the caption number label and number in the table of figures.

7. To right-align the page numbers, enable the Right Align Page Numbers option.

8. To use tab leaders, choose one in the Tab Leaders box.

9. Click OK to create the table of contents.

For more on tables of figures, see *Word For Windows 6 For Dummies.*

## Tables

Lets you organize numbers and text in columns and rows. Perhaps the main use of tables in Word for Windows is to construct financial rows and columns, but tables can also be used to arrange paragraphs side by side so that you don't need to press Enter at the end of each line and tab to each paragraph. (This early approach to side-by-side paragraphs is still used by a lot of people. The approach is sound until it comes time to modify the text. Then it's either time to go home sick or call a temp.)

Tables are constructed of *rows* (they run across the screen) and *columns* (they run up and down the screen). The box where a row and column meet is called a *cell.* You can put anything in a cell except another table. When you type in a cell, the text wraps within the cell, which is how side-by-side paragraphs work. When you first insert a table, regardless of the number of columns (up to 31), Word inserts the table from margin to margin, with each column being the same size. You can modify these settings after the table has been inserted. You can add and delete rows, columns, and individual cells. You can resize rows, columns, and cells individually. You can use decimal tabs within a table to align financial data.

If you want to get the full power of Word, start using tables. Almost everything you can do with a table can be found under the Table menu. The only exceptions are that you format text using the normal formatting procedures, and that you can add things like footnotes by using the normal footnote procedures.

## Creating a table

1. Place the insertion point where you want the table.

2. Click the Insert Table button on the Standard toolbar to see the table grid that appears just below the button.

3. Drag over the grid until you select the number of rows and columns you want in the table and release the mouse button.

4. Word inserts the table and places the insertion point in the first cell. You're ready to begin working in the table.

 You can also use Table⇨Insert Table to get the Table dialog box, where you can enter the number of columns and rows, change the spacing between columns, and format the table. In most instances, however, the method for creating a table described here will suffice.

 You can display or hide table gridlines by choosing Table⇨Gridlines. Whether or not you display the gridlines, they are still there.

## Using the Table Wizard

Microsoft has kindly provided a Table Wizard to help you create and format your tables in Word. You can use the wizard at first to help you create your table. As you gain proficiency with tables in Word, you will probably find that using the Table button on the Standard toolbar or the Table menu for your tables is quicker and more efficient.

1. Place the insertion point where you want to insert the table.

2. Choose Table⇨Insert Table to display the Insert Table dialog box.

3. Click the Wizard button to begin the wizard.

4. In the first Wizard screen, choose the table format. Choose Style 1 for no format. Click the Next button to continue.

5. In the next Wizard screen, choose the number of columns and any preset headings you want; then click Next to move to the next screen.

6. In the next Wizard screen, choose the number of rows and any present headings you want; then click Next to move to the next screen. (If you choose a preset heading like

Months of the Year, Word asks if you want the headings repeated on new pages and how you want the heading text formatted. Make your choices and then click the Next button. If Word takes you back to the question about Row Headings, just click Next again.)

7. In the next Wizard screen, define the cell contents. There are two options for numbers (right aligned and decimal tabs) and two options for text (left aligned and centered). Whatever you choose here applies to all the cells in the table, but you can easily change any cell formatting after you create the table.

8. In the next Wizard screen, choose the orientation of the table (portrait or landscape). If your choice is different from the document's page orientation, the wizard places the table on a new page and inserts section breaks before and after the table.

9. In the last Wizard screen, click Finish to create the table. Word inserts the table.

10. The Table Autoformat dialog box appears. Choose a formatting option from the Formats box and click OK.

## Moving in a table

To move to a cell in a table using the mouse, just click in that cell. The table that follows lists keystrokes for moving in a table.

| Move To | Keystroke |
| --- | --- |
| Next cell | Tab |
| Preceding cell | Shift+Tab |
| Next character within a cell | Right arrow |
| Previous character within a cell | Left arrow |
| Next row | Down arrow |
| Previous row | Up arrow |
| First cell in a row | Alt+Home or Alt+7 (Numeric keypad) |
| Last cell in a row | Alt+End or Alt+1 (Numeric keypad) |
| First cell in a column | Alt+PgUp or Alt+9 (Numeric keypad) |
| Last cell in a column | Alt+PgDn or Alt+3 (Numeric keypad) |

## Selecting in a table

Unlike Excel, Word doesn't permit you to select nonadjacent cells, columns, or rows at the same time.

There is a subtle difference between selecting text within a cell and selecting a cell itself. To select text within a cell, drag over the text. This distinction is important when you want to format the gridlines to print. If you select the text rather than the cell and use border formatting, the formatting applies only to the text and not to the cell gridlines.

### Selecting with the mouse

| To Select | Do This |
|---|---|
| A cell | Move the mouse pointer to the left of the cell until it becomes an arrow and then click. |
| A row | Move the mouse pointer to the left of the row outside the table and then click. |
| A column | Position the pointer on the top gridline of the column until it changes to a down arrow and then click. Or position the mouse pointer anywhere in the column, press Alt, and click. |
| Multiple cells, | Drag across the cells, rows, or rows, or columns columns. |

### Selecting with keystrokes

| To Select | Use This Keystroke |
|---|---|
| Contents of the next cell | Tab |
| Contents of the preceding cell | Shift+Tab |
| The entire table | Alt+5 on the numeric keypad |
| Adjacent cells | Shift+arrow key |
| A column | Place the insertion point in the top or bottom cell of the column. Press Alt+Shift+PgUp (if the insertion point is in the bottom cell) or Alt+Shift+PgDn (if the insertion point is in the top cell). |
| A row | Place the insertion point in the first or last cell in the row. Press Alt+Shift+End (if the insertion point is in the first cell) or Alt+Shift+Home (if the insertion point is in the last cell). |

# Inserting columns, rows, and cells

To insert columns, select the column or columns to the right of where you want the new column or columns. Then click the Table button on the Standard toolbar. Alternatively, choose Table⇨Insert Columns.

To insert rows, select the row or rows below where you want the new row or rows. Then click the Table button on the Standard toolbar. Alternatively, choose Table⇨Insert Rows.

When you insert cells, you can choose whether to shift the existing cells to the right or down. If you choose to shift the existing cells to the right, an extra cell (or more, if you selected more than one cell initially) is added to that row. If you choose to shift the existing cells down, an extra row (or more, if you selected more than one cell initially), not just a cell, is added to the table.

1. Select a cell or cells adjacent to where you want the new cell or cells.

2. Click the Table button on the Standard toolbar. Alternatively, choose Table⇨Insert Cells to display the Insert Cells dialog box.

3. Make the appropriate choice in the dialog box.

4. Click OK to close the dialog box and insert the new cell or cells.

# Deleting columns, rows, and cells

Deleting rows and columns works exactly the same as inserting rows and columns, except for two things: (1) you cannot use the Table button on the Standard toolbar (it only inserts); and (2) you choose Table⇨Delete rather than Insert. (The Delete command on the Table menu changes according to what is selected.)

You can also delete a row or column by first selecting it and then using the Cut button on the Standard toolbar or choose Edit⇨Cut. This method not only deletes the selection, but it also places it on the Clipboard so that you can paste it elsewhere.

You can delete the contents of a cell or the cell itself. To delete the contents of a cell, select them and press Delete. To delete a cell, select the cell and then choose Table⇨Delete Cells to display the Delete Cells dialog box. Make the appropriate choice and click OK.

# Changing column width

1. Select the column you want to adjust.

2. Choose Table⇨Cell Height and Width to open the Cell Height and Width dialog box.

3. Choose the Column tab.

4. Enter a value for the column width.

5. To move to another column, click the Previous Column or Next Column button.

6. When you have finished, click OK.

**TIP**

There are several methods for changing the width of columns in a table. Another method is to drag a column's gridline or one of the column markers in the ruler to adjust the column's width visually. When you use this method, the columns to the right of the selected column automatically adjust proportionally so that the overall width of the table doesn't change.

## Changing row height

1. Choose Table⇨Cell Height and Width to display the Cell Height and Width dialog box.

2. Choose the Row tab.

3. In the Height of Rows box choose either Auto, At Least, or Exactly. At Least allows you to set a value that specifies the smallest row height, but the row expands if the contents exceed that value. If you specify Exactly the row does not expand even if the contents exceed the value in the At box.

4. Enter a value in the At box. (If Height of Rows was set to Auto, entering a value in the At box changes the height to At Least.)

5. Click OK.

## Changing spacing between columns

1. Choose Table⇨Cell Height and Width to display the Cell Height and Width dialog box.

2. Choose the Column tab.

3. Enter a value in the Space Between Columns box.

4. Click OK.

# Moving and copying rows, columns, and cells

1. Choose the cells, rows, or columns that you want to move or copy.

2. Place the mouse pointer over whatever you selected until the pointer becomes an arrow pointing upper left.

3. To move the selection, click and drag. You can move the selection anywhere you want, including out of the table entirely. If you move it out of the table, the selection remains in the table format.

4. To copy the selection, press Ctrl and click and drag. As in step 3, you can copy the selection anywhere, including out of the table.

# Splitting a table

You can only split a Word table horizontally (by rows).

1. Position the insertion point in the row where you want the split to occur.

2. Choose Table⇨Split Table. Alternatively, press Ctrl+Enter (which not only splits the table, it inserts a page break, too).

# Formatting text in a table

Formatting in a table is exactly the same as formatting ordinary text. For character formatting, select the text and apply the formats. For paragraph formatting, place the insertion point in the paragraph and apply the formats. You can also apply styles to a table to automate the formatting.

# Centering a table

1. Select the table or rows you want to align.

2. Choose Table⇨Cell Height and Width to display the Cell Height and Width dialog box.

3. Choose the Row tab.

4. To indent the table, enter a value in the Indent From Left box. To center, choose Center in the Alignment box.

5. Click OK.

# Splitting and merging cells

1. Select the cells you want to split or merge.

2. To merge the selected cells, choose Table⇨Merge Cells. Word merges the cells, creating a paragraph for each paragraph in each merged cell. If the selected cells are all blank, the merged cell has no paragraphs.

3. To split the selected cells, choose Table⇨Split Cells to display the Split Cells dialog box.

4. Enter the number of columns you want to split the selection into. You can split cells that were not previously merged.

5. Click OK.

## Adding borders and shading to cells

The gridlines that appear when you create a table do not print. However, you can print borders for a table or for selected cells in a table. You can also shade selected cells. To apply preset border and shading formats to a table quickly, use the AutoFormat feature. To apply custom border and shading formatting, use Format⇨Borders and Shading.

1. Position the insertion point inside the table.

2. Choose Table⇨Table AutoFormat to display the Table AutoFormat dialog box.

3. Choose a format in the Formats box. A preview of the chosen format appears in the Preview box to the right.

4. Choose the elements you want to apply to the table in the Formats To Apply area.

5. In the Apply Special Formats To area, choose the parts of the table you want to have formatted.

6. Click OK.

## Sorting

1. Select the rows you want to sort.

2. Choose Table⇨Sort to open the Sort dialog box.

3. In the first Sort By box, select the first column you want to sort.

4. Under Type, choose Number, Text, or Date.

5. Choose Ascending or Descending order for the sort.

6. To sort one or two additional columns, repeat steps 3 through 5, using the Then By boxes.

7. If the table has a heading row that you don't want to include in the sort, choose the Header Row option under My List Has.

8. Click OK.

For more on sorting text, see **Sorting**.

## Numbering cells

1. Select the cells you want to number. To number only the first cell in each row, select the first column.

2. Click the Numbering button on the Formatting toolbar to open the Table Numbering dialog box.

3. Choose the numbering option you want.

4. Click OK.

## Calculating in a table

1. Position the insertion point in the cell where you want the answer to appear.

2. Choose Table⇨Formula to open the Formula dialog box.

3. If the suggested formula in the Formula box is not acceptable, select another one from the Paste Function box or enter one of your own. (For more on calculating in a table, see the Help topic "Performing Calculations in a Table.")

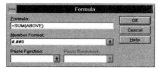

4. Select a number format if you wish.

5. Click OK.

## More stuff

In previous versions of Word, Calculations was a command on the Tools menu.

See **Tabs** for an explanation of using tabs in tables.

For more on tables, see *Word For Windows 6 For Dummies.*

## Tabs

Lets you set customized tab stops and leaders. A few words about tabs in general are in order, as this is a topic that confuses many users. Tabs, whether on a typewriter or in Word, consist of two elements: the *tab stop* and the *tab character,* which you insert by pressing Tab. You can use Word's preset tab stops or you can create custom tab stops of your own. Your custom tab stops can be formatted with tab leaders. (A *tab leader* is a solid, dotted, or dashed line that fills the space between the text and the tab stop.)

Most people get along fine with the default tabs. They are initially set every half inch, so that each time you press Tab the insertion point moves toward the right margin a half inch. You can set them to any interval, however.

## Changing default tabs

1. Choose Format⇨Tabs to open the Tabs dialog box.

2. Enter a value in the Default Tab Stops box. If you enter one inch, the default tab stops are set to one inch.

This is the only tab action that affects the entire document rather than a selected paragraph. The changes affect only the current document.

## Custom tab examples

In the examples that follow, you can see how each type of custom tab works. Each line has the same tab stop settings as the other lines. Left tabs align the text from the left, center tabs center the text under the tab stop, right tabs align the text from the right, and decimal tabs align on decimal. The numbers are formatted with decimal tabs and the vertical line at the end is formatted with bar tabs.

| Left Tab | Center Tab | Right Tab | 123.45 |
| Left Again | Center Again | Right Again | 1119.8 |
| Another Left | Another Center | Another Right | 21.988 |

## Tab leader examples

Dotted line tab leader ..................................................................... 10

Dashed line tab leader - - - - - - - - - - - - - - - - - - - - - - - - - - - - - - 10

Underline tab leader _____ 10

## Setting custom tab stops

When you set a custom tab stop, Word removes all the default tab stops in front of it so that you stop at the custom tab stop when you press Tab.

1. Select the paragraph you want to have the custom tab stops.
2. Choose Format⇨Tabs to open the Tabs dialog box.
3. Enter a value in the Tab Stop Position box. You can enter precise values, such as 2.025 inches.
4. Choose an alignment option under Alignment.
5. If you want a leader, choose the leader under Leader.
6. Click the Set button to set that tab. The dialog box stays open so you can set additional tabs.
7. When you have finished, click OK.

Removing a custom tab stop is a simple matter. Just select the paragraph that contain the tab stop and click and drag the tab stop right off the ruler.

You can quickly insert custom tabs along the ruler (except for bar tabs) with the mouse. First click the Tab Alignment button to the left of the ruler (it probably looks like an L) to choose the type of tab you want (left, center, right, or decimal). Each click of the Tab Alignment button changes it to the next alignment. Then click anywhere in the white space in the ruler to set the tab stop.

To get placement information about a custom tab stop in the ruler, press Alt as you click on the tab stop.

## Tabs and Tables

Sets custom tab stops and insert tabs in tables, even though the use of tables generally eliminates the need for using tabs. Just as in ordinary text, a tab operation in a table consists of two elements: the tab stop and the tab character which you type. In ordinary text you enter a tab in your text by pressing the Tab key, but in a table that moves you to the next cell. So to enter a tab in a cell press Ctrl+Tab. When you press Ctrl+Tab, you begin typing at the next tab stop in the cell, whether it is a default stop or a custom stop that you created.

You can enter a tab stop for a large number of cells at once by selecting the cells before entering the tab stop in the ruler. If you select cells in multiple columns, you must enter the tab stop in the ruler above the leftmost column that has a cell selected. (For example, if you select cells in the second, third, and fourth columns in the table, you must enter the tab stop in the ruler over the second column.) You can think of this as the *active column,* and it is indicated by the indentation markers in the ruler above that column. Word does not allow you to enter a tab stop in the ruler over any other column, whether it is selected or not.

Left, center, and right tabs work exactly the same in tables as they do in ordinary text except for the fact that you must press Ctrl+Tab to enter a tab character in a cell. However, decimal tabs work a little differently in tables because decimal tabs are most commonly used in tables that contain columns of numbers.

When you enter a decimal tab in the ruler over a selected column, the decimal tab takes effect immediately. There is no need to type a tab character in each cell. This is true whether the table contains text or numbers. As is true outside of tables, decimal tabs cause numbers to align on the decimal point. If some or all the numbers have no decimal point, they right-align. Text also aligns on the decimal tab as if it were a Right tab.

Using decimal tabs in a Word table creates a couple of problems. The first occurs if you enter more than one decimal tab in the ruler over a column or cell; the cell contents no longer aligns properly. The second is that, although you can enter a tab stop in the ruler only over the leftmost selected column or cell, you can drag the tab stop to adjacent columns, which also causes alignment problems.

The quickest and easiest way to correct either problem is to select the table, choose Format⇨Tabs, and click the Clear All button. This removes all custom tab stops in the table. You can then reapply the custom tab stops.

After you enter decimal tabs for a table, adjusting a column of numbers is simple. Just select the column (or multiple columns) and drag the tab marker in the ruler to the left or right. The column aligns under the tab wherever you place it.

## Templates

Lets you create a model that you can use for specialized documents. Each time you create a new file using File⇨New, you have the opportunity to choose a template to use as a basis for the new file. When you choose a template, Word opens a copy of that template. The copy includes text, macros, styles, AutoText entries and customized toolbars, menus, and shortcut keystrokes. Word comes with a number of predefined templates, which you can use or modify.

You can also create your own templates. When you create a new template, Word adds it to the list of templates you see when you create a new file. All templates have a DOT extension, which is how Word recognizes them as template files. It is important not to change the extension if you want to use that file as a template.

If you don't choose a custom template, Word uses the Normal template. The Normal template usually contains basic information, such as page size, margins, and the default font and font size.

# Creating a template from an existing document

1. Open the file.

2. Choose File⇨Save As to open the Save As dialog box.

3. Choose Document Template in the Save File As Type box. Word changes the the Template directory automatically.

4. Change the name if you like. Be sure not to change the file name extension (DOT); otherwise, Word cannot recognize the file as a template file.

5. Click OK to save the file as a template. Any text, macros, styles, and so on contained in the file are also part of the new template. Word closes the original file and leaves the new template open.

6. Make any changes you want to the new template; then save it and close it.

# Creating a template from an existing template

1. Choose File⇨Open to display the Open dialog box.

2. Switch to the Template directory.

3. Choose Document Template in the List Files of Type box to see a list templates.

4. Choose the template you want and click OK to open the template.

5. Choose File⇨Save As to open the Save As dialog box.

6. Type a new name in the File Name box. Be sure not to change the file name extension (DOT); otherwise, Word cannot recognize the file as a template file.

7. Click OK to save the file as a new template. Word closes the original template and leaves the new template open.

8. Make any changes you want to the new template; then save it and close it.

You can also create a new template based on another template by using File⇨New to open the New dialog box. Choose the template on which you want to base the new one; then choose the Template option under New and click OK. A new, unnamed template file opens with the same characteristics of the template you chose in the New dialog box. Make any desired changes and save the new template.

## *Using a template or wizard*

To use a template or wizard, choose File⎮Open to display the Open dialog box. Choose the template or wizard in the Template box and then click OK to create the new file.

## *Attaching a different template to your document*

1. Choose File⇨Templates to open the Templates dialog box.

2. Type the name of the template you want in the Document Template box.

3. If you aren't sure where the other template is located, click the Attach button to open the Attach Template dialog box. This box functions similarly to the File Open dialog box so that you can switch drives and directories to locate the other template.

4. If you want to update the styles in your document automatically when you attach the other template, enable the Automatically Update Document Styles option.

5. Click OK.

You can modify a template as you would any other Word document. Documents you created previously based on that template are not affected. To modify a template, choose File⇨Open, choose Document Template from the List Files Of Type box, choose the template, and click OK. Make the changes you want and save and close the template.

You can use the Organizer to copy elements of any template to any other template. For more on the Organizer, see **Organizer.**

## *Thesaurus*

Lets you replace a word or phrase with a synonym. Word also lists antonyms for some words. The thesaurus is a wonderful tool for those times when you feel you've overused a word and can't seem to find another similar word.

## For keyboard kut-ups

To open the Thesaurus, press

 + [F7]

## Using the thesaurus

1. Select the word you want to look up. If you don't select a word, the thesaurus looks up the word closest to the insertion point.

2. Choose Tools⇨Thesaurus to open the Thesaurus dialog box.

3. Choose the options you want.

## Toolbars

Use any of Word's toolbars or create your own as needed. Toolbars have buttons that you click to perform some sort of action. Word has eight built-in toolbars, plus other specialized toolbars that appear when you perform a certain function (such as headers and footers, print preview, and outlining). You can modify any of the built-in toolbars and create entirely new toolbars. You can also specify that the toolbar buttons display a label when you point at them (which is the default).

You can use two dialog boxes with toolbars: the Toolbars dialog box and the Customize dialog box. The Toolbars dialog box allows you to display and hide individual toolbars, as well as delete custom toolbars and reset built-in toolbars. The Customize dialog box allows you to modify any existing toolbar by adding and deleting button.

## Creating a custom toolbar

1. Choose View⇨Toolbars to open the Toolbars dialog box.

2. Click the <u>N</u>ew button to open the Toolbar Name dialog box.

3. Type a name for the new toolbar and choose the template where you want to store the toolbar.

4. Click OK to close the Toolbar Name dialog box. Word creates a new blank toolbar and opens the Customize dialog box with the <u>T</u>oolbars tab chosen.

5. Choose the <u>c</u>ategory that contains the items you want to add to the new toolbar.

6. In the next box, choose a button to see a description.

7. To add it to your new toolbar, just drag the button to the toolbar and drop it.

You can open either the Toolbars dialog box or the Customize dialog box quickly by pointing at any open toolbar and clicking the right mouse button to open the shortcut menu. Then choose either Toolbars or Customize from the bottom of the menu.

You can add a style, an AutoText entry, a font, a macro, or any command in Word to a toolbar. To make this change, scroll down to and choose All Commands, Macros, Fonts, AutoText, or Styles in the Categories box in the Customize dialog box. The center list box shows the appropriate options. Choose any item and drag it to your toolbar. If that item has a button assigned to it, Word automatically uses that button. If not, Word displays the Custom Button dialog box, where you can choose a button or type a label for the button in the Text Button Name box.

# Displaying and hiding toolbars

Choose <u>V</u>iew⇨<u>T</u>oolbars to open the Toolbars dialog box, and
deleting:

- To display a toolbar, click on the toolbar name to place an
  X in the box next to the toolbar.

- To hide a toolbar, click on the toolbar name to clear the X
  in the box next to the toolbar.

- You cannot delete a toolbar that comes with Word, but to
  delete a custon toolbar,  choose the toolbar you want to
  delete. When you click the Delete button, Word asks you to
  confirm the deletion. Click the Yes button and then click
  OK. Remember that once you do this, the custom toolbar is
  gone forever, as you cannot undo the deletion.

# Adding or deleting buttons on a toolbar

1. Be sure the toolbar you want to modify is displayed.

2. Point at the toolbar and click the right mouse button; then
   choose Customize from the shortcut menu. This opens the
   Customize dialog box.

3. To delete a button, just drag the button off the toolbar.

4. To add a button, choose the category that contains the item
   you want to add to the new toolbar. Then, choose a button
   (or command or style or the like) in the next box. To add it
   to your new toolbar, just drag it to the toolbar and drop it.

# Setting toolbar options

You can display color on the toolbar buttons (if your monitor is
capable of showing color), display the buttons as large or small,
and specify that Word display a description of a tool when you
point at it.

1. Choose <u>V</u>iew⇨<u>T</u>oolbars to open the Toolbar dialog box. Or
   point at any toolbar, click the right mouse button, and
   choose Toolbars from the shortcut menu.

2. To display color buttons, enable the C<u>o</u>lor Buttons option.

3. To display Large Buttons, enable the <u>L</u>arge Buttons option.
   You may want to display smaller buttons to fit more tools
   on the toolbar.

4. To have Word display a label when you point at a button,
   enable the <u>S</u>how Tool Tips option. You should really have
   this button enabled permanently, as it reduces the chance
   of clicking the wrong button.

## More stuff

Customizing toolbars is quick and easy in Word with no negatives. If you don't need the toolbar you created, just delete it. For more on customizing toolbars in Word, see *Word For Windows 6 For Dummies.*

## Typeover/Insert Mode

Lets you switch between the two modes. *Typeover mode* means that each character you type replaces (types over) an existing character. *Insert mode* means that each character you type moves existing characters to the right and down the page. Most people prefer to work in insert mode. Pressing Insert on the keyboard toggles you between the two modes. You can also double-click the OVR box in the status bar at the bottom of the screen.

## Underline

Underlines selected characters. Underlining is a character attribute, which means you first have to select the characters before you underline them.

See **Font Formatting** for more on this topic.

## For keyboard kut-ups

Select the text and press

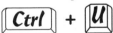

Ctrl + U

## For mouse maniacs

Select the text and click the Underline button on the Formatting toolbar.

## Underlining as you type

1. Click the Underline button on the Formatting toolbar or press Ctrl+U. All the characters you type will be underlined.

2. To turn off underlining, repeat step 1.

## Undo

Undoes your most recent actions. Word supports multiple levels of undoing and lets you choose how many previous actions to undo. There is also a Redo feature, so if you change your mind about undoing a series of actions, you can redo them quickly.

### For keyboard kut-ups

To undo one action at a time, press

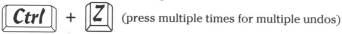 **Ctrl** + **Z** (press multiple times for multiple undos)

### For mouse maniacs

To undo a single action, click the Undo button once. To undo a series of actions, click the down arrow to the right of the Undo button to see a list of recent actions. Choose all the actions you want to undo.

## User Information

Enters User Information for Word to use in certain functions. For example, Word automatically enters the User Information as the return address when doing envelopes.

### Adding and editing user information

1. Choose Tools⇨Options to open the Options dialog box.
2. Click the User Info tab.
3. Add or edit user information as desired.

## Views

Lets you view your document in a number of different ways and magnifications. The table that follows lists views available from the View menu.

| View | Effect |
|------|--------|
| <u>N</u>ormal | Shows your document, but not headers, footers, multiple columns, footnotes, or endnotes. You can type, edit, and format in this view. |
| <u>O</u>utline | Shows the structure of your document. This specialized view is useful if you use Word's built-in heading styles for your headings. It allows you to collapse sub-heading so that you can quickly move through and rearrange your document. It is not a view for editing. |
| <u>P</u>age Layout | Shows the entire page, including headers and footers, multiple columns, footnotes and endnotes. The only drawback is its relative lack of speed in scrolling. |
| <u>M</u>aster Document | Shows a specialized view, similar to outline view. Used only when you work with master and subdocument. |
| <u>F</u>ull Screen | A view that hides everything but your text and an icon that lets you display the hidden items. You can still use the menus in this view if you know the shortcut keystrokes. |
| <u>Z</u>oom | Opens a dialog box where you can choose what magnification you want to use to view your document. Smaller magnifications display more of the document but are more difficult to view. |

Other specialized views are available. These views include print preview, header/footer view, and annotation view. Specialized views are covered under the specific topics in this guide.

## Wizards

Walks you through the chosen topic step by step. Wizards are automated routines developed to help you with the different features in Word. There are ten wizards in Word.

To use a wizard, choose File⇨New to open the New dialog box and then choose the wizard you want to use in the Template box and click OK. The wizard takes you through creating the object step by step.

## *WordArt*

Lets you create text designs and text shapes that aren't otherwise available. You can create WordArt in place in your document; the WordArt tools and menus are available while you work on the WordArt text.

## *Creating objects in WordArt*

1. Position the insertion point where you want to insert the WordArt object.

2. Choose Insert⇨Object to open the Object dialog box.

3. Click on the Create New tab. The WordArt toolbar and menu bar appear and you can begin creating the WordArt object. If you had previous versions of Word for Windows installed on your computer, both WordArt 1.0 and 2.0 will be listed; otherwise, only WordArt 2.0 is listed. Double-click the 2.0 version.

4. Type the text you want to format in the Enter Your Text Here box.

5. Use WordArt's menus and tools to modify the text. For help with step-by-step instructions, press F1.

6. When you have finished, click in any part of your Word document to close the WordArt toolbar and change the menus back to the Word menus.

## *More stuff*

Because objects created in WordArt are embedded objects, all you need to do to edit such an object is to double-click on it.

WordArt may seem complex and confusing at first, but it is actually quite easy to use. Use the step-by-step instructions to guide you through the various parts of the toolbar. Also, for more on using WordArt, see *Word For Windows 6 For Dummies.*

WordArt is one of three supplementary applications to help you add special text effects, equations, and charts to documents. The other two are Equation Editor and MS Graph. These applications all use object linking and embedding, or OLE. For more on these topics, see **Equation Editor, Graph, Inserting Objects,** and **OLE.**

# Zoom

Lets you view your document in different magnifications. Word allows you to view a document anywhere from 25% to 200% of size.

## For mouse maniacs

Click the Zoom Control button on the Standard toolbar to change magnifications.

## Zooming in and out on your document

1. Choose View⇨Zoom to open the Zoom dialog box.

2. Choose the view you want.

# Notes

# Notes

# IDG BOOKS WORLDWIDE REGISTRATION CARD

RETURN THIS REGISTRATION CARD FOR FREE CATALOG

**Title of this book:** Word for Windows 6 for Dummies Quick Reference

**My overall rating of this book:** ❏ Very good [1]  ❏ Good [2]  ❏ Satisfactory [3]  ❏ Fair [4]  ❏ Poor [5]

**How I first heard about this book:**

❏ Found in bookstore; name: [6]

❏ Advertisement: [8]

❏ Word of mouth; heard about book from friend, co-worker, etc.: [10]

❏ Book review: [7]

❏ Catalog: [9]

❏ Other: [11]

**What I liked most about this book:**

**What I would change, add, delete, etc., in future editions of this book:**

**Other comments:**

**Number of computer books I purchase in a year:**  ❏ 1 [12]  ❏ 2-5 [13]  ❏ 6-10 [14]  ❏ More than 10 [15]

**I would characterize my computer skills as:**  ❏ Beginner [16]  ❏ Intermediate [17]  ❏ Advanced [18]  ❏ Professional [19]

**I use**  ❏ DOS [20]  ❏ Windows [21]  ❏ OS/2 [22]  ❏ Unix [23]  ❏ Macintosh [24]  ❏ Other: [25] _____
(please specify)

**I would be interested in new books on the following subjects:**
(please check all that apply, and use the spaces provided to identify specific software)

❏ Word processing: [26]

❏ Data bases: [28]

❏ File Utilities: [30]

❏ Networking: [32]

❏ Other: [34]

❏ Spreadsheets: [27]

❏ Desktop publishing: [29]

❏ Money management: [31]

❏ Programming languages: [33]

**I use a PC at** (please check all that apply): ❏ home [35]  ❏ work [36]  ❏ school [37]  ❏ other: [38] _____

**The disks I prefer to use are**  ❏ 5.25 [39]  ❏ 3.5 [40]  ❏ other: [41] _____

**I have a CD ROM:**  ❏ yes [42]  ❏ no [43]

**I plan to buy or upgrade computer hardware this year:**  ❏ yes [44]  ❏ no [45]

**I plan to buy or upgrade computer software this year:**  ❏ yes [46]  ❏ no [47]

Name: _____  Business title: [48] _____

Type of Business: [49]

Address ( ❏ home [50]  ❏ work [51] /Company name: _____ )

Street/Suite#

City [52] /State [53] /Zipcode [54]: _____  Country [55] _____

❏ **I liked this book!**
You may quote me by name in future IDG Books Worldwide promotional materials.

My daytime phone number is _____

**IDG BOOKS**

THE WORLD OF COMPUTER KNOWLEDGE

**YES!**
Please keep me informed about IDG's World
of Computer Knowledge. Send me the latest
IDG Books catalog.

NO POSTAGE
NECESSARY
IF MAILED
IN THE
UNITED STATES

## BUSINESS REPLY MAIL
FIRST CLASS MAIL     PERMIT NO. 2605     SAN MATEO, CALIFORNIA

*IDG Books Worldwide*
*155 Bovet Road  Suite 310*
*San Mateo  CA 94402-9833*